DAYS OUT WITH KIDS

1995/96 EDITION

To Owain, born October 4th, 1994
despite all his attempts to distract me.

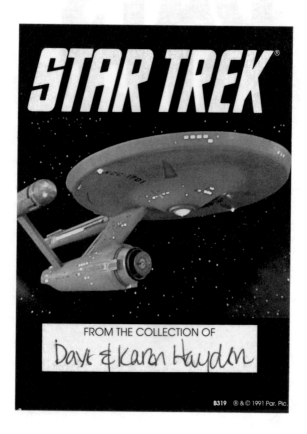

FROM THE COLLECTION OF

Dave & Karen Hayden

B319   ® & © 1991 Par. Pic.

DAYS OUT WITH KIDS

1995/96 EDITION

Great Days Out in the South East for people with young children

Janet Bonthron

TWO HEADS
PUBLISHING

First published in 1995 by

Two Heads Publishing
12A Franklyn Suite
The Priory
Haywards Heath
West Sussex
RH16 3LB

ISBN   1-897850-01-8

Book design by Lance Bellers
Cover design by Don McPherson
Illustrations by Sam Toft

Printed & bound by Caldra House Ltd., Hove, Sussex

Contents

Animal Encounters
Farms, Zoos And The Like

Up, Down, There And Back
Trains And Fairs

The Great Outdoors
Gardens And Attractions

Look! Look! Look!
Exhibitions And Things To See

Somewhat Historical
Castles, Cottages And Commoners

The Sun Has Got His Hat On
Walks And Picnic Spots

Introduction

WELCOME TO THE SECOND EDITION OF 'DAYS OUT With Kids'. Full of ideas for trips out with young children, it has been expanded to include many new trips around London, and with updated information on trips included in the first edition.

As a mother of young children I know how important it can be to get out of the house at times. Equally, it is often difficult to think of places to go, which are not too far, and where children will be well catered for. This book helps you tackle those problems, by offering you my personal selection of great outings to go on with young children.

My aim has been to describe outings which we all enjoyed as a family, that is with something to interest adults as well as children. A few places are really adult outings, but which if you take children they will enjoy the day too, although maybe not in the same way as the adults! I hope that most of them are new to you, and introduce you to some unusual, fun places we have been.

Each of the outings has been personally visited by us. Some are old favourites many times visited. Others are recommendations by friends of places they love. We have noted what facilities are provided for people with young children, for example whether high chairs are available, what the nappy changing facilities are like, whether it is easy to walk around with a pushchair, and how generally amenable it is for energetic and truculent young children! Many places have excellent child-friendly facilities, and others have less good. However, places haven't been selected for inclusion purely on the basis of facilities. Rather I have followed the ☛

principle that, if you know in advance what is there, you can plan accordingly and still enjoy the day. To sum up, each of the places included are in the book because we had a fun day there, and I think that other people with young children could too.

A note on the ages of children covered. The book is aimed at people with children from babies to about five or six years old. I would guess that most of the outings included would also appeal to older children, (many have lots of space, information boards and quizzes etc.) but I haven't specifically checked.

We visited these places in the winter just as much as summer. It is worth remembering that although many places are lovely in warm weather it is just as possible to have a trip out in the winter and autumn as in spring and summer, and often less crowded.

The facts given for each place have been checked rigorously. However, things do change, and I must stress the need to check details (particularly opening times) before you set out.

The views and opinions describing each outing are very much personal thoughts and reactions: inclusion does not constitute an endorsement. All the trips were done anonymously.

I should love to receive your comments on any places you visit in this book. Equally, any outings you think should have been included. Please send them to me at Two Heads Publishing – the address is on the Feedback page at the end of the book.

Janet Bonthron

How To Use This Book

EACH SECTION OF THE BOOK COVERS TRIPS WHICH FALL into the same broad category of attraction. Outings are described alphabetically within the section. If you know what sort of outing you want to do, then just look at the section titles, read the section summaries below, and flick through the entries included in that section. Alternatively, the handy planning guide is a rapid, self-explanatory table for identifying the right trip for you.

ANIMAL ENCOUNTERS covers trips to farms, zoos and other birds and beasties type places. Small children and animals are a winning combination, and there are plenty of places around London which offer it. I have chosen those which I think are distinctive in some way, for example superb handling opportunities for children, wonderful setting, or unusual or imaginatively-displayed animals. Try them all for variety!

Animal Encounters

UP, DOWN, THERE AND BACK has steam train ride outings, and a steam fairground. Puffs of steam and the smell of smoke in the air are always thrilling for young children and the ones I have included have features which make them particularly accessible. Eat your heart out, Thomas the Tank Engine!

Up, Down, There And Back

THE GREAT OUTDOORS is about trips which are all or mostly outdoors in character, in an especially beautiful or quiet setting. Ideal for walks and strolls, with plenty to see for adults whilst the little horrors run around exhausting themselves. Couldn't be better! ☞

The Great Outdoors

Look!
Look!
Look!

LOOK, LOOK, LOOK! features places with exhibitions or displays which young children should particularly enjoy, be they a busy airport runway (Gatwick), a pint-sized town (Bekonscot), or nose-to-nose contact with deep-sea creatures (Brighton Sea Life). These outings offer the chance for children to see something unusual or to experience at close quarters something they may only have seen on television.

Somewhat
Historical

SOMEWHAT HISTORICAL attractions all have a bygone age theme. Your children may not fully appreciate the historical connotations, but will be able to enjoy the setting and exhibits, whilst you can wallow in romantic nostalgia!

The Sun
Has Got
His Hat On

THE SUN HAS GOT HIS HAT ON includes picnic spots that are obviously just a small selection of what is available. Most good picnic spots tend to be closely guarded secrets, but these are ones which are favourites of ours. There is something about spreading your blanket on the ground and unpacking boxes and plates of picnic food that is just pure summertime, and you can't beat it. Happy munching! Of course, many of the locations in sections one to five are also excellent picnic spots.

IF, ON THE OTHER HAND, YOU DON'T MIND WHAT SORT of attraction you go to, but have other criteria (such as the weather, distance, or means of transport for example) which you need to satisfy, then the best way to use the book is to refer to the map and planning guide given on the following pages. These should help you to pick a suitable day out.

The planning guide can help you select an outing by travel time, prevailing weather, accessibility by public transport, or opening hours. Travel timings are approximate, and taken from Central London.

The planning guide also indicates whether opening periods are restricted (i.e. if a place is not open all the year, and/or only on some days of the week). I have erred on the generous side when deciding on the wet weather suitability - if you don't miss too much by ducking inside somewhere during an occasional shower then I have classified it as 'wet weather suitable'. Likewise, I have been quite liberal in interpreting public transport accesssibility, and for some outings you may need to take a short taxi ride (I do say in the Fact File given for each attraction if this is the case).

Once you have identified a trip that sounds appealing, refer to the detailed description for further information. Page numbers are given in the table. The Fact File which accompanies each entry gives the address and telephone number, travel directions and distances, opening times and prices, and an indication of specific facilities (high chairs, nappy change areas, and eating places). Where appropriate, the Fact File also suggests other nearby attractions.

Map

Animal Encounters

1 Badsell Park Farm
2 Birdworld
3 Bocketts Farm Park
4 Chapel Farm
5 Cotswold Wildlife Park
6 Drusillas Zoo Park
7 Lockwood Donkey Sanctuary
8 Loseley Park Farm
9 Wimpole Home Farm & Hall
10 Woodside Farm & Wildfowl Park

Up, Down, There And Back

11 The Bluebell Railway
12 Colne Valley Railway
13 Hollycombe Steam Collection & Gardens
14 Leighton Buzzard Railway
15 The Watercress Line

The Great Outdoors

16 Bentley Wildfowl & Motor Museum
17 Blenheim Palace
18 Claremont Landscape Gardens
19 Hatfield House
20 Penshurst Place
21 The Whitbread Hop Farm
22 Wisley Royal Horticultural Society Gardens

Look! Look! Look!

23 Bekonscot Model Village
24 Brighton Sea Life Centre
25 Didcot Railway Centre

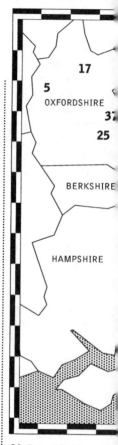

5
17
OXFORDSHIRE
37
25
BERKSHIRE
HAMPSHIRE

26 Gatwick Airport & Zoo
27 Kempton Park Races
28 Knebworth House
29 Syon Butterfly House & Park

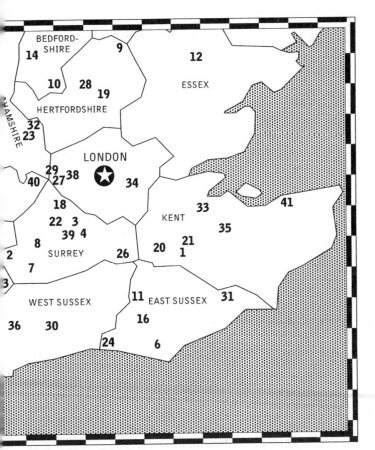

Somewhat Historical

30 Amberley
Industrial Museum
31 Bodiam Castle
32 Chiltern Open
Air Museum
33 Fort Luton &
Kent Life Museum
34 Greenwich –
Cutty Sark
& Maritime
Museum
35 Leeds Castle
36 Weald &
Downland Open
Air Museum

The Sun Has Got His Hat On

37 Clifton Hampden
38 Kew Gardens
39 Polesden Lacey
40 Windsor Town
& Great Park
41 Whitstable

Planning Guide

OUTING	Travel Time	OK in wet weather?	Public Transport	Opening	Page
ANIMAL ENCOUNTERS *Farms, Zoos And The Like*					
Badsell Park Farm	1 hr 30 mins	✓	✓	restricted	19
Birdworld	1 hr 15 mins	no	✓		22
Bocketts Farm Park	50 mins	✓	✓		25
Chapel Farm	45 mins	no	✓	restricted	28
Cotswold Wildlife Park	2 hrs	no	no		31
Drusillas Zoo Park	1 hr 30 mins	✓	✓		35
Lockwood Donkey Sanctuary	1 hr	no	✓		38
Loseley Park Farm	45 mins	✓	no	restricted	41
Wimpole Home Farm & Hall	1 hr 30 mins	✓	no	restricted	44
Woodside Farm & Wildfowl Park	1 hr	no	✓	restricted	48
UP, DOWN, THERE AND BACK *Trains And Fairs*					
The Bluebell Railway	1 hr 30 mins	✓	✓	restricted	51
Colne Valley Railway	1 hr 30 mins	✓	no	restricted	55
Hollycombe Steam Collection & Gardens	1 hr	✓	✓	restricted	59
Leighton Buzzard Railway	1 hr	no	✓	restricted	62
The Watercress Line	1 hr 30 mins	✓	✓	restricted	65
THE GREAT OUTDOORS *Gardens And Attractions*					
Bentley Wildfowl & Motor Museum	1 hr 30 mins	no	no	restricted	68
Blenheim Palace	1 hr 45 mins	no	no	restricted	72
Claremont Landscape Gardens	30 mins	no	✓		76
Hatfield House	45 mins	no	✓	restricted	79
Penshurst Place	1 hr 15 mins	no	✓	restricted	83
The Whitbread Hop Farm	1 hr 30 mins	no	✓		86
Wisley Royal Horticultural Society Gardens	30 mins	no	no		89

OUTING	Travel Time	OK in wet weather?	Public Transport	Opening	Page
LOOK! LOOK! LOOK! *Exhibitions And Things To See*					
Bekonscot Model Village	50 mins	no	✓	restricted	92
Brighton Sea Life Centre	1 hr 30 mins	✓	✓		96
Didcot Railway Centre	1 hr 30 mins	no	✓	restricted	99
Gatwick Airport & Zoo	1 hr	✓	✓		102
Kempton Park Races	45 mins	no	✓	restricted	106
Knebworth House	1 hr	✓	✓	restricted	110
Syon Butterfly House & Park	30 mins	✓	✓		113
SOMEWHAT HISTORICAL *Castles, Cottages And Commoners*					
Amberley Industrial Museum	1 hr 30 mins	no	✓	restricted	116
Bodiam Castle	1 hr 30 mins	no	no		120
Chiltern Open Air Museum	45 mins	✓	✓	restricted	123
Fort Luton & Kent Life Museum	1 hr 30 mins	no	no	restricted	126
Greenwich – Cutty Sark & Maritime Museum	45 mins	✓	✓		130
Leeds Castle	1 hr 30 mins	no	✓		134
Weald & Downland Open Air Museum	1 hr 30 mins	✓	✓	restricted	138
THE SUN HAS GOT HIS HAT ON *Walks And Picnic Spots*					
Clifton Hampden	1 hr 30 mins	no	no		141
Kew Gardens	45 mins	no	✓		144
Polesden Lacey	45 mins	no	✓		148
Windsor Town & Great Park	1 hr	no	✓		151
Whitstable	1 hr 30 mins	no	✓		155

If the Opening column is blank for a particular entry, it means that attraction is generally open every day, all year round

Badsell Park Farm

THIS IS A WELL-RUN SMALL FARM THAT THOUGHTFULLY offers several other attractions besides the usual farm animals that young children enjoy so much! It is in an attractive valley in Kent, complete with picture-book oast house, brick farm house, rolling fields and woodland. Although it is possibly more fun in the summer, when you can go fruit picking, the indoor play facilities and farm walks mean that it is also a good trip in spring or autumn.

The farm is set in fruit fields, including strawberries, raspberries, blackberries, gooseberries, Old English apples and pears. In season, you can pick-your-own (or pick-eat-your-own, in our daughter's case!) Be prepared for smeary fingers, and a modest amount of somewhat squashed fruit from your little

> **"Pigs are always good value with children because they make such a noise!"**

darlings! Meanwhile, you can get on with the serious business of picking... Alternatively you can buy the fruit at the farm shop, but that is less fun.

The Animal Park is home to a number of traditional farm animals, such as goats, ponies, sheep, pigs, cows, as well as geese, chickens and ducks. They live in a grassy enclosed park area, with a small pond and stream running through. The walk around the Animal park is fenced – so there is no ☞

Kids really love close contact with animals – the noisier the better!

danger of falling in the water - but access to the animals is a bit restricted. Pushchairs can easily be pushed around. Some animals are in enclosed sheds, where you can get a close look. When we were there the pig shed had seven five-day-old piglets, as well as other older ones. Pigs are always good value with children because they make such a noise! There is also a small pet area, with lots of different types of rabbits and guinea pigs, though with limited handling.

The walk through the Animal Park ends in a super open play area, with a real fire engine! As you can imagine, this has high entertainment potential. The play area also boasts a well-designed wooden fort, complete with climbing ropes and bridge over the stream. Nearby there is a large, covered sandpit and a ball pond.

Tractor rides run from just outside the Animal Park entrance (check at the entrance for times), for a 15-minute lurch around the fields in a covered trailer. Buggies can be accommodated. Pony rides are also available, although not on all days. Both tractor and pony rides cost an extra 60p per person (including toddlers). For the more energetic, there are two farm walks available, one about a mile in length, and a shorter one of about half a mile. These both go through fields and ancient woodland, with plenty of wildlife and wildflower interest. They can be muddy after rain and not really suitable for pushchairs.

Animal Encounters

A cafe and gift shop are in the oast house, and you can get a good range of hot food, sandwiches, cakes and cream teas. The barn next door has great indoor play facilities for up-to-six-year-olds, and birthday parties can be catered for here. There are also picnic areas, including one in a covered barn.

FACT FILE

Address: Badsell Park Farm, Crittenden Road, Matfield, Tonbridge, Kent

···

Telephone: 01892 832549

···

Directions: From Sevenoaks take the A21 south towards Tunbridge Wells. Take the Pembury road off the A21, and the farm is signposted from the roundabout at that exit

···

Public Transport: By train from Charing Cross to Paddock Wood, and taxi from the station (about 2 miles)

···

Distance: 44 miles **Travel time:** One and a half hours

···

Opening: From the end of March to November every day, from 10.00am-5.30pm

···

Prices: £3.00 adults, £2.50 children three and over, under-threes free. Farm trail and fruit-picking free

···

Nappy changing facilities: ✓ **Restaurant facilities:** ✓

···

High chairs: ✓ **Dogs:** No **Pushchair-friendly:** ✓

···

Nearby: Whitbread Hop Farm (see page 86)

Birdworld

"Who's a pretty boy then?"

IF YOU OR YOUR CHILDREN LIKE BIRDS, BIRDWORLD IS A must. Even if you're not bothered about them, it is still a stimulating and unusual day out, amidst pleasant garden surroundings. It is really a zoo for birds, with all sorts of different species – colourful and otherwise – on display and displaying themselves in enclosures and cages. The downside is that, being birds, handling potential by eager little people is limited, if not downright dangerous (ref. the vultures!). However, there is plenty to see, hear and pick up, indeed at home we are still admiring the display of blue, red and gold feathers we collected from the ground whilst we were there.

> **"Penguin Island is home to about 30 penguins and has a very good underwater viewing enclosure"**

The cages and enclosures are well set-out along paths which are easily negotiable with pushchairs. Some enclosures have hedging round them which can be a bit high for toddlers to see over, although there are often holes in the hedge for peering through! However, most of the birds can readily be seen, especially those in the cages. Some, like the ostrich, are quite friendly (or curious?), so you can see them at close quarters. At over seven feet tall the ostrich was rather too daunting a prospect for my daughter, who took refuge behind my knees!

There are birds from all over the world. For our children, highlights were the noisy squawking parrots with their bright plumage, the laughing ducks, flamingos and pelicans on the lake, and, of course, Penguin Island. This is home to about 30 penguins, and has a very good underwater viewing enclosure, which lets you see the birds diving and playing underwater. Penguin feeding at 11.30am and 3.30pm is great fun. If you book in advance you can feed them yourself and the £5 charge is donated to charity.

Animal Encounters

Other special features include the seashore walk (terns and oyster catchers), the woodland trail (native birds and trees), and the tropical walk (exotic birds in a heated environment). The 30-minute talk in the Heron theatre (hourly during the summer, 1.00pm only in winter), with live appearances from Birdworld inhabitants is worth looking in on.

The small Jenny Wren farm is also very appealing to youngsters. This has farm animals (goats, pigs, horses, chickens, doves etc.), of which some are roaming around freely, although I'm not completely sure if that was intentional! On our visit there was much hilarity chasing the rabbits, which tantalisingly hopped a few feet away every time we tried to stroke them.

Exhibits range from the very short to the very tall!

There is also a road train ride, (50p for a 10-minute round trip, running weekends from Easter, and ☞

weekdays during summer school holidays), and a good children's playground with slides, swings and climbing paraphernalia. This is next to a large picnic area with tables, benches and cafe facilities, as well as toilets with nappy-changing bench. There is another cafe and an ice-cream parlour, plus more toilets and a small gift shop at the entrance.

Adjacent to the Birdworld entrance is Underwater World, housing a small display of freshwater and marine fish. This provides a useful wet weather diversion.

FACT FILE

Address: Birdworld, Holt Pound, Farnham, Surrey
....
Telephone: 01420 22140
....
Directions: A3 to Guildford, and then the A31 (Hogs Back) to Farnham. Signposted from the end of the Hogs Back dual carriageway. Alternatively, signposted from junction 4 of the M3
....
Public Transport: Train from Waterloo to Aldershot (six mile bus ride), Farnham (three mile taxi ride) or Bentley (one and a half mile signposted walk through forest)
....
Distance: 40 miles   **Travel time:** About an hour and 15 minutes
....
Opening: 364 days a year from 9.30am. Closing 6.00pm in summer, and 4.30pm in winter
....
Prices: £3.95 adult, £2.25 children. Under-3's free. Family £11.50. Underwater World £1.20 adult, 60p children
....
Nappy changing facilities: ✓   **Restaurant facilities:** ✓
....
High chairs: ✓   **Dogs:** No   **Pushchair-friendly:** ✓
....
Nearby: Birdworld is set in the Alice Holt forest, which has trails and picnic areas suitable for pushchairs. Near to Frensham Ponds

Bocketts Farm Park

Animal Encounters

IF YOU THINK YOU'VE HAD ENOUGH OF SQUELCHING around muddy fields, trailing after elusive chickens or rabbits, well, think again, because Bocketts is really very good, being extremely well-equipped to deal with young children (and their hard-pressed carers). Although justifiably popular, it is rarely crowded. You can even have a good time there in the rain (we have done!).

One of the best features of the farm is that the animals are very accessible to children. They are mostly kept in small enclosures in a very large open barn, and within the barn there is a mélange of different creatures – when we last visited there were greedy goats, sleepy calves, squealing piglets, sheep, a donkey and an enormous Shire horse in residence. Because it is a working farm different animals are inside the barn depending on the time of year: spring is good time for lambs, when you can see ☛

A wonderful Noah's Ark of farm animals roam freely in the large barn

them being born or bottle-fed. There is a separate area at the back of the barn for smaller animals – rabbits, guinea pigs, ducklings and chicks, all watched over by loud-crowing cockerels. All the animals are very friendly and children are encouraged to feed, touch, stroke, and generally admire them. Bags of feed are on sale at the entrance for 25p a bag. Farm staff are around to talk to, and there are loads of information plaques everywhere, to allow you to bolster your reputation for omniscience. There is plenty of space for pushchairs between the different enclosures.

> **"All the animals are very friendly and children are encouraged to feed, touch, stroke, and generally admire them"**

Outside the barn there is also a lot to see and do. Tame and beautiful red deer live in a small area next to the barn. You can follow a short walk on a broad path (suitable for pushchairs) around the fields to see horned cows, billy goats and more pigs. The shaggy water buffalo is very friendly. At weekends, and during holidays and the summer there are tractor trailer and pony rides (small extra charge). There is also a great playground with old tractors to climb on, an enormous sand pit, hay bales and a two storey Wendy house as well as swings, slide and a wooden adventure area and trim trail (as if young children need any more exercise!). On occasions it can be muddy – don't wear your best shoes!

If they tire of the playground and/or it is pouring with rain, the hay bale 'castle' back in the barn is a very popular alternative, with bales to scramble all over and under. Even crawling babies can enjoy playing with the hay.

When you've had enough you can retire to the spacious and attractive 18th century barn which serves homemade lunches and teas. There is a children's menu, lots of high chairs (mostly with straps), and a small play area with toys. On sunny days nobody seems to mind if some of the toys migrate outside to the large yard. Lunch cost us about £5.00 a head (which included both adult and child's portions). The tearoom will cater for birthday parties (£2.65 per child), or you can bring your own party food and use the barn for £10.00. If you want to picnic there are both covered and open areas outside with tables and benches.

Animal Encounters

The gift shop is well-stocked and sells lots of farm books and toys, as well as the more usual gifts.

FACT FILE

Address: Bocketts Farm Park, Young Street, Fetcham, Nr Leatherhead, Surrey

Telephone: 01372 363764

Directions: Take A3 and A24. Signposted from the Leatherhead roundabout on the A24

Public Transport: Train to Leatherhead or Fetcham from Waterloo, and short taxi ride

Distance: 20 miles **Travel time:** 50 minutes

Opening: All year. 10.00am-6.00pm

Prices: Adult £2.40, children (3-17 years) £1.75, children (2 years) £1.00, under 2's free. Reduced rates Mon-Fri in term times

Nappy changing facilities: ✓ **Restaurant facilities:** ✓

High chairs: ✓ **Dogs:** No **Pushchair-friendly:** ✓

Nearby: Polesden Lacey, a National Trust house and gardens (see page 148)

Chapel Farm

THIS IS A FRIENDLY, SMALL FARM WHICH IS EASY TO GET to, not far from London. It has the usual range of farm animals, which are well displayed for small people, and plenty of opportunities for handling and stroking. For older children, there are lots of informative notices and displays. As it is a working sheep farm, in the summer you may be lucky enough to see sheep shearing going on, and all through the year there are usually lots of baby animals to admire.

A great place to get to know the animals as well as you want, in an uncommercialised setting

Most of the animals to see are kept in pens and barns surrounding a traditional farmyard, replete

with scratching chickens and noisy ducks cavorting in a muddy farm pond. Fencing prevents eager duck-chasers from enjoying splashing in the mud themselves! There are several varieties of pigs, including some of the friendliest we have seen – our 11-month-old was pretty intrigued by his encounter with a Berkshire sow. When we were there Lucy, the proud mother of six piglets, obliged us by prodding them awake with her snout, so we got a good view.

Animal Encounters

The walk around the farmyard takes about an hour and a half, depending how often you accept the invitation to get in the pens with the animals. Calves, sheep, and goats with huge floppy ears are waiting for you, as well as a Shire horse and Shetland ponies. The lovely Chapel Barn is home to a pair of Barn Owls, but they must have been

"In Flint Barn we saw the thrilling spectacle of a chick emerging from its shell"

asleep when we were there. In Flint Barn, which is full of ducklings and chicks, we saw the thrilling spectacle of a chick emerging from its shell. As usual, rabbits and guinea pigs were squealingly popular. If you visit the rabbits at feeding time you can get in and feed them carrots.

Behind the farmhouse there is a lovely play area – a good manageable size, with a Land Rover, tractors and huge tractor wheels to play on, and sunny benches so you can rest whilst keeping your eye on your children. Various small farm animals, notably ducks and chickens share the play area.

Don't come to the farm for lunch, unless you bring your own. Refreshment facilities are limited to vending machines with snacks and drinks. However, there are plenty of lovely sites for a picnic, with benches and tables. You could also shelter in the Honeysuckle Barn for your picnic if you needed to, and the children can also amuse ☛

themselves playing hoop-la there.

As well as the farmyard, there is a farm trail through a beautiful wooded valley, with views of nearby Box Hill. This takes about 45 minutes, but could be difficult with a pushchair after wet weather (check in advance). If you don't fancy walking, tractor trailer rides leave half-hourly for a 30-minute trip to the farm boundaries (£1.00 each person). Pony rides are often available for a small extra charge too, with hard hats provided. All in all, quite enough to keep you and young children amused for a day!

FACT FILE

Address: Chapel Farm, West Humble, Dorking, Surrey

Telephone: 01306 882865

Directions: The farm is just off the A24 Dorking road between Leatherhead and Dorking. Take the right-hand turning off the A24 just beyond the Burford Bridge roundabout, signposted to Boxhill Station. The farm is about a mile along this road

Public Transport: Train to Boxhill and Westhumble from Waterloo (via Clapham Junction). About half a mile walk along the road (narrow and no pavements) to the farm

Distance: 20 miles   **Travel time:** 45 minutes

Opening: Every day mid February to November. 10.00am-6.00pm

Prices: £1.70 adults and children. Under-2s free

Nappy changing facilities: ✓   **Restaurant facilities:** No

High chairs: No   **Dogs:** ✓ on leads   **Pushchair-friendly:** ✓

Nearby: Box Hill has lovely walks and space to run about. The King William pub on the opposite side of the Mole valley has good food and gardens. Note though there is limited room for families inside

Cotswold Wildlife Park

"Tyger! tyger! burning bright
In the forests of the night
What immortal hand or eye
Could frame thy fearful symmetry?"

Animal
Encounters

COME HERE TO SEE WILD ANIMALS THAT YOU CAN'T SEE on a farm – real tigers, rhinos and zebras to name a few, in 120 acres of gardens and landscaped parkland around a large Gothic style manor house. However, it is a long way to go so an early start and careful timing to coincide with sleep periods are advised. On the positive side though, it does offer a varied, exciting day out and is just as much fun in winter as summer, so the trip really is worth it.

Despite being terrified of the tiger (well, who wouldn't be?) our children had a wonderful day here. On arrival we headed straight for the real wild animals – the leopards, tiger and rhinos. Well-signposted paths radiate out from the car park, so you can easily work out which way to go. Passing what looked like some random tor stones, which suddenly moved towards us, we admired the giant tortoises. Despite wanting to ride on them, our daughter was tempted away with promises of more things to come.

> **"Cotswold offers a varied, exciting day out and is just as much fun in winter as summer"**

After a short walk past a vast apparently empty field we came to the zebra house, leopard house, and most spectacularly the tigers. Obviously zebras and leopards aren't stupid (it was a cold day) – they were all inside, but the large glass windows in their houses, with steps up for children, meant we could all get a wonderful view of them. No such ☞

shivering inside for the tigers – they were prowling around looking highly ferocious, but the close up sight of those sharp yellow teeth, glinting eyes and huge paws (even safely behind wire netting) proved too much for our daughter and we had to beat a hasty retreat to the relative safety of the Bactrian camels.

Back around the house there are plenty more animals to see – red pandas, monkeys, gibbons and emus are just some of what is on offer. They are all very well displayed, with ditches and viewing platforms enabling you to get a really close up look. To be within six foot of a white rhino is quite an experience and our son was clearly enthralled, although we were not able to persuade him that it wasn't a "dawg"! There is also a children's farmyard area, with a good display of pot-bellied pigs, angora goats, rabbits, guinea pigs, ducks and poultry. Some of these may be stroked and petted, and they are very accessible for small children to see and appreciate.

The house and attached buildings contain a number of other attractions, including the reptile and invertebrate houses, and aquarium. Warm, with subdued lighting and suitably impressive slimies and slitheries, these proved very popular, although children have to be lifted to see inside some displays. The bat house, where you can look down on the bats swirling below you, was fascinating. It adjoins the glass animal house, where you can see a myriad of miniature glass animals both on display and being made.

Other areas to visit are the walled garden with otters, meerkats, toucans, and hornbills. Many more birds, including flamingoes, cranes, swans and ducks can be seen in the lake area. You are not allowed to feed them though. All the paths are easily accessible to pushchairs, including those round the lake, and there are plenty of good, clear information boards and signs.

Behind the house is an adventure playground with slides, swings, climbing equipment and other amusements for children from babyhood to at least eight-years-old. The helter-skelter is quite awe-inspiring and very popular with five-year-olds. I should expect the playground could get crowded in busy periods. There is also a narrow gauge railway – trains are always fun – which runs at 20-minute intervals from April to October inclusive and takes you on a good-value tour of the whole park past most of the animals' enclosures (£1.00 charge per person).

The park is very well-served with picnic areas, with a large picnic lawn in front of the ☞

Animal Encounters

You can get an extremely good look at very spectacular animals – such as tigers!

house, and picnic tables in several other locations, including the adventure playground. There is a large self-service cafe, with a highly distracting baby dinosaur display (lizards to you and me). High chairs with straps are provided, but were in rather short supply. Half of the seating area is non-smoking. There is also a bar, with seating outside as well as indoors.

During the summer there are many special events, including birds of prey flying demonstrations, car rallies, morris dancing, and archery tournaments. All in all a great many things are on offer – try it!

FACT FILE

Address: Cotswold Wildlife Park, Burford, Oxon

Telephone: 01993 823006

Directions: Oxford exit from the M40. Take the Oxford ring road north (signposted A40 Cheltenham), then the A40 to Burford. The park is signposted from the A40

Public Transport: None

Distance: 80 miles   **Travel time:** 2 hours

Opening: 10.00am-6.00pm or dusk, whichever is earlier. Open every day except Christmas Day

Prices: £4.60 adults, £3.00 children over four. Under-4 free

Nappy changing facilities: ✓   **Restaurant facilities:** ✓

High chairs: ✓ limited   **Dogs:** ✓ on leads

Pushchair-friendly: ✓

Nearby: Oxford, Blenheim Palace (see page 72), Cogges Farm Museum at Witney (01993 772602)

Drusillas Zoo Park

Animal
Encounters

THE ANIMALS AT DRUSILLAS HAVE ALL BEEN SELECTED for their appeal to young children. The zoo lives up well to its own description as 'the best small zoo in the country', both in terms of the child-sized animals there and the compact, manageable area to walk around. However, don't be mistaken, there is certainly a lot to see – we spent a full day there, amid shrieks of pleasure, and had the added benefit of very sleepy children on the way home! It was very popular when we went though, (during the school holidays) and correspondingly very hectic.

The zoo is imaginatively laid-out, with a succession of different themed areas – evolution, farm animals, climbing animals and monkeys, Australian outback, Beaver country, Wind in the Willows, to name a few. Participation and understanding of the animals are encouraged with lots of brain-teasers, quizzes and physical 'tests'. For example, the children are invited to try hanging like a monkey on poles, milking a very life-like cow, or running as fast as a llama on all-fours. All the animals may be viewed easily by toddlers, and there is plenty of space for them to run around, and to manoeuvre a buggy. You can even crawl into one of the enclosures through a tunnel and pop up

> **"The zoo lives up well to its own description as 'The Best Small Zoo In The Country'"**

inside a large dome for real eyeball to eyeball contact with a troop of Meerkats (small furry rodents with long necks). The displays are great fun and really brought the zoo to life. Quite a lot of parent interaction is called for though, so if you are feeling particularly jaded – be warned!

Events such as feeding periods, or times when staff get in the cages and 'play' with some animals, and special attractions, for example, the baby ☞

DOWN ON THE FARM!

The zoo has been well-designed to help children relate to the animals

animals, are well worth a look. The staff are easily recognisable in red 'Drusillas' tee-shirts and trousers: those we spoke to were very friendly and helpful. During the school holidays and weekends animal handling sessions (rabbits and guinea pigs) are held (see notice at gate for times).

Other attractions are an acre of play areas including a toddler tumble, an under-six-year-old tumble room, a general play area with an SAS style extension, and an indoor playbarn – useful on a rainy day. These are busy during the school holidays, but highly tempting for children, containing a customised tractor, fire engine and wooden houses to play in and on. There are two trains in operation offering trips around the park, but queuing time to get on a train was about 20 minutes when we were there. Grey Owl's barn in Beaver Lodge offers a special exhibit on conservation and is worth a look.

There is a choice of several places to eat and an area for you to enjoy your own picnics. The Inn at the Zoo is open at all times and has hot and cold lunches. Toucans Restaurant is open weekends and school holidays during the week, with lots of high chairs. The Inn at the Zoo offers pub food and teas, and has a restful and quiet garden, with live music and plenty of space for children to tire themselves out running around.

Animal Encounters

Several shops are dotted about – including a gift shop, toy shop, fudge factory, and wacky workshop. About a third of the zoo is under cover, so it would be possible to go in wet weather.

FACT FILE

Address: Drusillas Park, Alfriston, East Sussex

....

Telephone: 01323 870234

....

Directions: Take the M23/A23, and then the A27 to Lewes. Follow the A27 on towards Polegate, and Drusillas is signposted off at the Wilmington roundabout

....

Public Transport: Train to Polegate from Victoria or Clapham Junction, with a good taxi service from the station (3 miles)

....

Distance: 54 miles   **Travel time:** 1 hour 30 minutes

....

Opening: Daily throughout the year, except Christmas and Boxing Days. Open from 10.00am-5.00pm in the summer (last admission), and until 4.00pm in the winter

....

Prices: Adults £5.20, children £4.50, under-3's free

....

Nappy changing facilities: ✓   **Restaurant facilities:** ✓

....

High chairs: ✓   **Dogs:** No   **Pushchair-friendly:** ✓

....

Nearby: Brighton (see the Look!Look!Look! section). The Alfriston Heritage Centre (01323 870303) has a blacksmith's museum, historical exhibition and lovely walks

Lockwood Donkey Sanctuary

TRY A VISIT HERE IF YOU ARE FEELING UNLOVED. WITH a bucket of scrubbed carrots on your arm (available at the shop for £1.00) the 160 donkeys will go out of their way to make you feel welcome, and you will definitely be very popular! Young children seem to be untiringly thrilled by close encounters with animals, and Lockwood gives plenty of opportunity to get to know the donkeys, who all are very gentle and friendly. So friendly, in fact, that my daughter hardly murmured when she was nudged into a puddle on her bottom by an over-enthusiastic beast.

> **"Lockwood gives plenty of opportunity to get to know the donkeys, who all are very gentle and friendly"**

Located in a beautiful wooded part of Surrey, the Sanctuary is a home for several other sorts of rescued animals, besides donkeys, cared for in a peaceful, rural environment. (Peaceful, that is, apart from the squeals of delight from young visitors as their carrots are efficiently removed from them). There are goats, horses (also keen on carrots), pigs, dogs, a wallaby, Holly the deer and at least one llama. Plus the usual squawking geese, ducks, and chickens that you come to expect on these days out. All the animals can be visited in stables and fields which surround a large traditional farmyard, complete with authentic steaming manure! You are free to wander around the farmyard, and we had no trouble taking a buggy everywhere.

There is an 'adopt a donkey scheme' which costs £1.00 for children, £2.00 for adults, and gives you a certificate and regular newsletters.   ☛

Donkeys are surprisingly gentle – despite their greedy enthusiasm our little boy quite happily kept the carrot supply going

Facilities are somewhat limited. There are loads of picnic tables and rudimentary toilets, and the shop sells some drinks, souvenirs and stickers (as well as second-hand books and clothes, and, of course, carrots). During the summer and at Christmas there are special event days when more is on offer – stalls, teas and animal parades. Apart from these days, it is probably a good idea to combine a visit to Lockwood with another attraction, for example Wisley Gardens (see The Great Outdoors section), or see the suggestions in the Fact File.

FACT FILE

Address: Lockwood Donkey Sanctuary, Farm Cottage, Hatch lane, Sandhills, Wormley, Near Godalmimg, Surrey

....

Telephone: 01428 682409

....

Directions: Take the Haselmere turn off the A3, and follow the A283 Petworth road, before turning right to Sandhills at Wormley. The Sanctuary is three quarters of a mile from the A283 turnoff, signposted down a rough road on the left

....

Public Transport: Train to Witley station, and a 10-minute walk along a footpath (ask at the station for directions)

....

Distance: 38 miles   **Travel time:** 1 hours drive

....

Opening: All year. 9.00am-5.30pm or dusk

....

Prices: Free, donations welcome

....

Nappy changing facilities: No   **Restaurant facilities:** No

....

High chairs: No   **Dogs:** ✓ on leads   **Pushchair-friendly:** ✓

....

Nearby: Walks on Sandhills Common (National Trust). Painshill Park (01932 868113). The White Hart pub at Whiteley (meals and children's playground). Guildford Leisure centre (01483 444777)

Loseley Park Farm

LOSELEY PARK IS A BEAUTIFUL ELIZABETHAN HOUSE set in a 1,400 acre estate, consisting of gardens, woodland, and, of course, pasture for the famous Loseley Dairy herd. No need to remind ice-cream connoisseurs that the renowned Loseley dairy products are made here! Although you can visit the splendid house (45-minute guided tours, pushchairs not admitted), the main attraction for those with youngsters in tow is the chance to be shown around a working dairy farm. The grounds are also fabulous, with great walking potential, and you are able to picnic in some lovely spots. At the edge of the car park there is a covered open barn with benches and tables, which is ideal for picnics, especially in damp weather.

The farm tours run in the afternoons (from about 12 noon), and start with a tractor trailer ride. This is covered and large enough to take a pushchair complete with sleeping baby! The ride was very popular with our toddlers, bumping and jolting us slowly down from in front of the house to Orange Court Farm. On the way you pass some of the 165 Jersey cows belonging to the estate: beautiful, elegant beasts with liquid brown eyes.

At the farm, there is plenty of opportunity to get to know the herd better. You can visit the

> **"If you time your trip right you can actually watch the cows being milked"**

bulls with rings in their noses (Jerseys are reputedly the fiercest bulls around!), stroke some of the many calves, and go into the milking shed. If you time your trip right (about 3.30pm) you can actually watch the cows being milked, eight at a time. Other animals on the farm include pigs, rare poultry, ☞

A tractor trailer ride takes you down to the farm and brings you back

and 43 different varieties of sheep. Our helpful guide willingly delved into the chicken run to rescue black and white spotted guinea fowl feathers for the children to have, and handed out handfuls of soft sheep's wool to be taken home. The tour lasts just over an hour, and returns you, on the trailer again, back in front of the house. Although the farm visit was a bit muddy (wellies recommended), it is all negotiable with pushchairs.

Have tea in the tithe barn to the right of the house. This serves reasonably-priced wholefood cakes, snacks, hot food and drinks, is lovely and large, and has a wooden floor ideal for crawling children. There is a limited number of high chairs. The shop sells Loseley products (don't forget to bring a cool bag), as well as home-baked bread. There is a nappy changing area in the spacious ladies toilets at the back.

The newly-opened nature trail is a one mile walk through the woods, lovely at all times, but especially in May, when the ground is covered with bluebells. It is probably too rough for pushchairs though. Finally, the walled gardens at the side of the house are also worth a visit. The moat walk there is lovely, but toddlers will need watching because of the open water in the moat. The rambling old mulberry tree in the gardens, with branches hanging right down to the ground is particularly noteworthy in late summer when it is covered with delicious, squashy berries. Watch out for tell-tale stains on fingers and clothes!

Animal Encounters

FACT FILE

Address: Loseley House, Compton, Nr Guildford, Surrey

....

Telephone: 01483 505501 or 01483 304440

....

Directions: Signposted off the A3, just beyond Guildford

....

Public Transport: None

....

Distance: 30 miles   **Travel time:** 45 minutes

....

Opening: May to September. Wednesday to Saturday 2.00pm-5.00pm. Grounds open from 11.00am. Restaurant and shop 11.00am-5.00pm. House closed on Sundays

....

Prices: Grounds and farm trailer ride £4.00 adults, £2.00 children; house, grounds and trailor ride combined £5.40 adults, £3.15 children. Under-3's free

....

Nappy changing facilities: ✓   **Restaurant facilities:** ✓

....

High chairs: ✓(limited)   **Dogs:** No   **Pushchair-friendly:** ✓

....

Nearby: Lockwood Donkey Sanctuary (see page38). Guildford Leisure Centre with swimming pool and creche

Wimpole Home Farm & Hall

"**W**AGONS, PIGS AND TRACTORS" WOULD SUM UP Wimpole in the eyes of our children, I think. This beautifully-restored architect-designed late Georgian farm is owned by the National Trust and lies in the grounds of one of their properties, Wimpole Hall. For adults it offers a fascinating view of the way farms used to be – though I suspect a lot cleaner than in reality! – whilst for children there are plenty of animals and farm vehicles to admire.

Take a wagon ride down to the farm from the stableblock near the main house. Pulled by two enormous Shire horses, this authentic farm wagon is covered and gives a surprisingly smooth ride, with good views of the parkland and grounds surrounding Wimpole Hall. It costs an extra 60p per person (under-3's free) one way, and takes about 10 to 15 minutes. Our children loved the scramble up the wagon steps, the ride itself, and the enormous friendly horses.

Coming into the farm you are immediately ☛

The Victorian farm has a wagon museum and rare breed of farm animals

Animal Encounters

struck by the smell of good old farmyard manure, and hordes of squawking, flapping geese and chickens. The usual fun can be had by children admiring them (well, chasing, actually). The farm is laid out around a traditional yard, with rare breeds of cattle in the centre, and other animals in the surrounding barns and sheds. These handsome buildings are all wooden, several have thatched roofs. The children will be more impressed by the animals I expect: rare breeds of pigs, goats, and horses. There were no less than three litters of piglets when we visited, so you can imagine the squeals of excitement (from all parties!). The pens are all arranged so that even toddlers can get a good view, except for the Shire horse who was unsociably hidden away in his stable on our visit.

The wagon museum is full of restored old painted wagons, barrows and carts. They give a romantic glimpse of rural life in the late eighteenth and nineteenth centuries — you can almost hear the dancing round the Maypole.

"There were no less than three litters of piglets when we visited"

Other attractions include a rabbit barn, a short walk past fields of sheep and goats, a wooden adventure play area in the woods, and a play area with real and toy tractors, surrounded by picnic tables. There is also a duck pond – suitably green and slimy – with picnic tables adjacent too.

Facilities at the farm are a bit limited – portacabin loos with no nappy changing, a shop, and a small refreshment area in one of the barns. More facilities are back up in the stableblock and main Hall. You can either get the wagon and horses to take you back there, or have a gentle 10-minute stroll through the 1790's pleasure gardens.

The Hall grounds are very extensive, consisting of

lovely wooded parkland ("Capability Brown woz 'ere"), with mature trees, woodland, a folly, bridges and small lakes. There are several waymarked walks through the park, ranging from one and a half to five and a half miles in length. Pick up a walks leaflet in the stableblock (donation requested). Dogs must be kept on leads.

Animal Encounters

There are several special events in both the farm and Hall. Look out for the lambing weekends at the farm in March, and costume fairs, craft fairs and fun days held throughout the year.

FACT FILE

Address: Wimpole Hall & Home Farm, Arrington, Royston, Herts

Telephone: 01223 207257

Directions: Off the A603, 8 miles SW of Cambridge. Follow the Wimpole Hall sign from the A11 or A1198 junction with the A603

Public transport: Nearest train station is 5 miles away at Shepreth

Distance : 55 miles **Travel time:** 1 hour 30 minutes

Opening: Daily from March to October, except Mondays (but including Bank Holiday Mondays). The Hall is closed Fridays too. Farm open 10.30am-5.00pm, Hall 1.00pm-5.00pm (from 11.00am on Bank Holidays). The farm is open weekends only in winter months

Prices: Farm and grounds £3.75 adults, £2.00 children. Under-3's free. Hall £4.50 adults, £2.00 children. Combined ticket £6.00 adults, £3.00 children. Reduced prices for National Trust members

Nappy changing facilities: ✓ in stableblock only

Restaurant facilities: ✓　**High chairs:** ✓

Dogs: No (except Guide Dogs)　**Pushchair-friendly:** ✓

Nearby: RSPB bird sanctuary at Sandy (0767 680551)

Woodside Farm & Wildfowl Park

WOODSIDE'S OFFICIAL NAME REALLY DOESN'T DO the place justice – it doesn't indicate either the scale or the comprehensive nature of the facilities. However it's reasonably compact with a good mix of indoor and outdoor facilities and so is a great place to go on those days when you're not quite sure whether it's going to rain or shine. But do be warned, it isn't open on Sundays.

More than just a farm; a huge range of different birds, and plenty of hungry chickens to feed!

We visited on a Monday when it was very quiet with a few other toddler and carer groups pottering around like us. Perhaps because it was so quiet we had the impression that the whole enterprise was staffed by about three people who kept dashing from coffee shop to farm shop to attractions as their

customers moved around: this didn't matter in the least as no-one was in a great hurry and it did add to our amusement!

Animal Encounters

Woodside is set in six and a half acres of woodland and feels very extensive, despite a three hour stay we didn't get all the way round. This was partly because our children were diverted by the play area with its 'Tarzan Trail' which kept them busy for a good half an hour enabling us to catch up on conversation as we watched from the picnic table.

> "Special events are held regularly – Easter Egg Scrambles, Morris Men and Circus Tricks to name but a few"

There are over 150 species of farm animals and wildfowl here. As far as animals are concerned, there were two big hits for us: firstly there was James, an extremely hungry goat (bags of food are on sale for 25p!), and secondly there were some pigs wallowing in some quite glorious mud which of course meant that the children had to share in the experience and get as muddy as possible! Other animals include horses, donkeys, sheep, cattle and poultry.

There is a huge range of different wildfowl and we enjoyed them as the children threw food. Older children would probably enjoy the barn egg grading and packing display in the large barns. There is also a barn largely populated by rabbits, which interested our young children but the smell left something to be desired by the adults! Luckily we were able to escape to embark on a tractor trailer ride around the site, an activity laid on each day, at a small extra cost. On Saturdays and during the school holidays there are also pony rides. Special events are held regularly – Easter Egg Scrambles, Morris Men and Circus tricks days to name but a few.

All of the layout, range of animals, style of presentation and upkeep of the farm are impressive and make it an easy day out for grown ups with no ☛

chance for children to get bored. The coffee shop offers sandwiches and some hot food although you'll need the second door opening if you arrive with a double buggy otherwise you won't get in! There are also lots of picnic areas, both indoors and outside. The farm shop isn't brilliant for little ones, or rather for their carers, as a lot of things are displayed very low down providing endless opportunities for taking things off shelves. Likewise nappy changing facilities are limited, a small room at the entrance to the ladies loo with a little shelf!

FACT FILE

Address: Woodside Farm Shop and Wildfowl Park, Mancroft Road, Slip End Luton, Beds
....
Telephone: 01582 841044
....
Directions: Take the A5 towards Dunstable from the M1 junction 9. Turn right after 2 miles, onto the B4540 to Luton, following the brown tourist signs to the farm
....
Public transport: Train to Luton, then short taxi ride (about £2.50)
....
Distance: 35 miles   **Travel time:** 1 hour
....
Opening: Monday to Saturday 8.00am-5.30pm all year except Christmas, Boxing and New Year's Days
....
Prices: Adults £1.60, children £1.20, babies under 6 months free
....
Nappy changing facilities: ✓   **Restaurant facilities:** ✓
....
High chairs: ✓   **Dogs:** No
....
Pushchair-friendly: ✓
....
Nearby: Stockwood Country Park in Luton has a craft museum, and the Mossman collection of horse-drawn vehicles, with daily rides through the park

Up, Down, There And Back
Trains And Fairs

The Bluebell Railway
"The Engineer said he rang the bell
And she blew, Whoo-oo-oo!"

THERE WILL BE ENOUGH BELLS RINGING, STEAM hissing and smoke blowing down on the Bluebell Line to satisfy even the most ardent Thomas the Tank Engine enthusiast. For older train-spotters, a trip on the Bluebell Railway really conjures up the mythical Golden Age of steam – a time when to travel by train was an excitement and a pleasure in its own right, and trains ran on time! (ponder on this next time you squash onto the 7.49). Be warned though, it can be very busy at peak weekends (avoid Mother's Day!). However, it does run all year, so it is a good trip to do in the winter, and is a good option in wet weather.

"Children will love the thrill of doors slamming, whistles blowing and the guard waving his green flag"

It consists of a reclaimed stretch of railway line running between Sheffield Park Station (near Haywards Heath) and East Grinstead. Volunteers have lovingly amassed a wonderful collection of old steam trains and station memorabilia, and you can take rides up and down the line in old Southern Region carriages pulled ☞

by restored steam trains.

You can join the train at Sheffield Park station, Horsted Keynes the next station on the line, or at Kingscote. If you start at Kingscote you need to catch the specially-provided 1950's bus from East Grinstead station – a 10-minute ride that will immediately get you into the authentic feel of things! We started from Sheffield Park where coal fires laid during the winter in the Booking Office and waiting-room, add to the nostalgia created by the unmistakeable cokey smell of steam trains which is all around. The station is a bustling flurry of people and announcements as the trains arrive and depart. Be prepared to mingle with an incongruous mix of hordes of delighted children and and anoraked train-spotters.

Rituals are re-enacted with careful attention to detail

There is plenty to see at the station, but we decided to get straight on a train and were treated to a dose of instant nostalgia. Remember that smoky smell of brown velveteen seats, sliding windows you can just manage to peep out of, and mirrors in the carriages where you could check your first attempts at make-up? Children will love the thrill of doors slamming, whistles blowing and the guard waving his green flag, before the train chugs slowly along through beautiful Sussex countryside. Watch out for sheep and horses in the adjoining fields.

The trip to Horsted Keynes station takes about 15 minutes. The station is an authentic re-creation of the bygone heyday of the railways, complete with a coffin carrier, and mounds of leather-bound suitcases and trunks. You can get off there for a look round, good views of the comings and goings of trains and carriages, or for walks in the woods (good for bluebells in May). Alternatively you can go five miles further on to Kingscote station which is newly restored and reopened, and where a picnic area is being developed.

Back at Sheffield Park station, there is plenty to amuse young children. Stroll over the iron footbridge and look down on the engines busying backwards and forwards, or stopping to be refilled with water from an enormous water pipe. On the opposite platform there is a small museum of train and station memorabilia, and a model railway of Horsted Keynes in the 1920's (weekends and Wednesdays only). Take a peep into the gleaming signals box with labelled handles, and walk right alongside the locomotives, watching the fires being stoked and the pistons throbbing, before, with smoke pouring, they slowly pull out of the station.

At the rear of the station is the engine workshop, where you can walk between the rails right next to the collection of huge locomotives and carriages. Impressive sounding banging and scrapings were coming from the renovation section when we were there. It all adds to the atmosphere!

Restaurant and cafe facilities are good. At Sheffield Park station you have the choice of a reproduction Victorian pub, serving meals and with a full bar (real ales served), or the Puffers self-service cafe upstairs, which has hot and cold meals, snacks, and drinks. There were only two high chairs though. At Horsted Keynes there is an original 1882 station buffet, again with a full bar service. If you feel like lashing out, Pullman carriages on Sunday trains offer lunches or cream teas (no high chairs on trains).

Alternatively, there are some picnic spots near the stations and picnic tables next to the platforms at all the stations. There is a small platform shop at Sheffield Park which sells a host of train ☞

items – toys, books, videos, crockery etc., as well as basics such as films, guide books and postcards.

Trains run at intervals of between 45 and 90 minutes , depending on the time of year and day, so it is worth checking times in advance if you do not want to hang about too much. A round trip takes about an hour and a half.

Special events held during the year include a steam gala (extra trains laid on), a vintage transport fair, and in 1995, special 35th birthday celebrations in August.

FACT FILE

Address: The Bluebell Railway, Sheffield Park Station, Nr Uckfield, East Sussex

Telephone: 01825 723777 (bookings and enquries) 01825 722370 (24 hour information)

Directions: M23 and A23,leave at the junction with the A272 at Bolney. Follow the brown Bluebell Railway signs from there

Public Transport: Train to Haywards Heath, with bus connections to Sheffield Park running most Saturdays, some Sundays and some weekdays through the summer (ring the number above for details)

Distance: 45 miles   **Travel time:** 1 hour 30 minutes

Opening: Weekends throughout the year. Weekdays from the beginning of May to the end of September, plus during Easter week, last week in October, and Christmas week. Ring in advance to check timetable

Prices: Admission and return trip, adult £7.00, children £3.50, family (2 adults, 3 kids) £19.00. Under-3's free

Nappy changing facilities: ✓   **Restaurant facilities:** ✓

High chairs: ✓   **Dogs:** ✓   **Pushchair-friendly:** ✓ (80p charge)

Nearby: Sheffield Park Gardens, about a mile away, are beautiful National Trust gardens. Not open in the winter.

Colne Valley Railway
". . . fings ain't wot they used to be!"

IF A TASTE OF LUXURY APPEALS TO YOU, VISIT THIS reconstructed railway. Although as you approach it the view of clapped-out trains and decrepit railway equipment may lead you to think that you have arrived at the wrong place. A short walk from the parking area, past the yet-to-be-repaired trains, to the lovingly restored station puts to rest any such doubts. Here you will find all the steam trains, Pullmans and carriages to keep even the youngest train enthusiast (or not-so enthusiast!) entertained for several hours.

Located in a delightful, secluded spot in Essex countryside, the Colne Valley Railway is the vision of two railway fans who wanted to re-create the atmosphere of a typical Essex country branch line of yesteryear. Built and staffed entirely by volunteers, it consists of Castle Hedingham station, a working signal box, and a mile of track which once formed part of the Colne Valley and Halstead Railway. Every effort has been made to make the railway authentic, with the buildings, bridges and working signalbox modelled or re-constructed from local stations and railways. Castle Hedingham station, for example (which now houses one of the two gift shops) was moved brick by brick from its original site.

"Pride and joy must be the Pullman, consisting of three historic carriages in luxurious Orient Express style"

The train stock held by the railway includes eight steam trains, nine diesels, and a multitude of passenger carriages and wagons. Not all have yet been restored, but there are at least three ☛

There is always plenty going on at the station on steam days, and lots of people to talk to!

working steam engines, two diesels, and one diesel railbus – enough to satisfy even the busiest Bank Holidays.

During the open season trains run on steam days between 12noon and 4.00pm for a 20-minute round trip. Make sure that you check in advance which are steam days if you want a ride. With only one mile of track, the train ride itself is a bit short and uneventful, although you can do as many return trips as you like for your entrance money! Nevertheless, it is a very pretty trip, running through woodland and along the banks of the River Colne, with all the usual steam, flags and whistles. The engine drivers are there to talk to and you can see the signal box in operation.

On non-steam days the entrance fee is reduced, and all the carriages, engines and buildings are open for viewing. Children can climb up onto the engines (if you don't mind how dirty they get!), and you can walk along the track. The staff are extremely helpful and willing to provide extra information on the history and running of the trains.

Pride and joy of the fleet must be the Pullman train though. It consists of three historic carriages in luxurious Orient Express style, including a first-class restaurant offering Sunday lunches. Lunches have to be booked in advance. However, it may be difficult to justify all afternoon at the dining table to your children, who will probably be more keen to explore than eat. Some other time, maybe! We took the less luxurious, but more child-friendly option of the buffet car facilities at the station, where you can get light snacks and drinks in a more convenient atmosphere, albeit with a less sumptuous menu. There is also a picnic area in the adjoining four and a half acres of woodland, with tables in the summer, from where you can watch the trains roll by.

Plans are afoot (or awheel?) to expand the railway. Planned developments include an engine shed, a workshop, a museum, a station display area, and improved visitor facilities. These are subject to planning permission, and are unlikely to be ready in 1995. Current toilet facilities are modest at best (there are no toilets available on the trains, so be warned before you embark). Likewise, be prepared to lug your pushchair up the steps of the passenger bridge to cross the tracks. You'll probably find the buggy isn't really necessary anyway – best to let little legs tire themselves out running up and down the platform, and have a peaceful journey home yourself, whilst your youngster dreams of being a railway engineer!

Special events planned for 1995 include Teddy Train days (bring a teddy) and Goldilocks and the Bears (try to spot them), as well as Santa Specials at Christmas.   ☛

For a really worthwhile day out, try a visit to nearby Castle Hedingham castle as well. This ruined Norman keep, overlooking the picturesque medieval village, has grassy grounds ideal for picnics, and 100 acres of peaceful woodland and lakeside walks. Children can have great fun exploring inside the castle, which has narrow stairs and windows. The interior is too inaccessible for pushchairs though. There are some indoor seating areas, and teas are offered, but we'd recommend returning to the railway for a cream tea and some more train rides!

FACT FILE

Address: Colne Valley Railway, Castle Hedingham, Halstead, Essex

Telephone: 01787 461174

Directions: Exit 8 from the M11, then the A120 to Braintree, and follow the A131 towards Halstead. Signposted from Halstead, five miles north west on the A604 Cambridge to Colchester road

Public transport: None

Distance: 60 miles **Travel time:** 1 hour 30 minutes

Opening: Open all year 10.00am-5.00pm for non steam days. Steam days every Sunday from mid March to the end of October, and mid week at Easter, half terms, and during the summer

Prices: Steam days £4.00 adults, £2.00 children, under-2's free. Family tickets £20.00. Half price on non-steam days

Nappy Changing facilities: No **Restaurant facilities:** ✓

High chairs: No **Dogs:** No **Pushchair-friendly:** No

Nearby: Castle Hedingham castle (01787 60261)

Hollycombe Steam Collection & Gardens

"Mind You Hold On Tight!"

IT WAS TEEMING WITH RAIN, AND WE ONLY HAD ONE pair of wellies between four of us. With drips running down our necks we resolutely struck out towards the fairground. Groups of overall-clad enthusiasts with coal-smeared hands and smutty faces were busy around several huge gleaming engines. Furnaces roared, smoke billowed, and pistons trembled. Suddenly with a tremendous "Tralalala, Bombom, Bombom, Boom-Babaa!" a fairground organ burst into life. We were at the funfair!

Hollycombe is a brilliant day out. Despite the rain we had a marvellous time. There is lots to do and to chose from. First there is the fairground, with about eight different, traditional rides: galloping horses carousel, big wheel, razzle dazzle tilt wheel, and steam yachts, to name a few. Our toddler went on some of these, but really loved the juvenile rides (strict notices informed us that adults are not permitted on these!), where she was spoilt for choice on the roundabout between the fire engine with ladder and bell, double decker bus or airplane (she 'compromised' by having a go on all three). Luckily, the entry ticket enables you to have unlimited numbers of rides.

> **"Hollycombe is a brilliant day out. There is lots to do and to chose from"**

When you want a change from the fairground, there are no less than three different train rides to pick from. The longest is a mile and a half ride on a narrow gauge railway, pulled by the locomotive 'Jerry'. This passes through woodland, along a ridge with wonderful views of the South Downs, and ☛

Persuading kids – or adults – to get off the rides can be a problem

even through a tunnel. Then there is a miniature railway, with its own station and clock tower, and finally, the huge 'Commander B' locomotive (lots of puff and whistles), which pulls two carriages along a short standard gauge railway. All these rides offer protection from the rain in covered carriages.

There is also a steam tractor and trailer which takes you down to the farm, where you can see a plough and working steam farm equipment, as well as some real farm animals. For steam fans there are other engines too.

Finally, there are the gardens: mostly woodland, with great views, and wonderful azaleas and daffodils in the Spring, where you can go for a lovely walk whilst your children explore. Only limited access with pushchairs though.

Although the steam equipment doesn't get going until 2.00pm, you can go in earlier to walk in the gardens or have something to eat in the covered cafe. This offers basic refreshments such as drinks, sandwiches, pasties etc. No high chairs though. Of course, there are plenty of good picnic spots, including the car park. The gift shop sells souvenirs, toys, postcards, and general train items. Parents of Thomas the Tank engine fans beware!

Up, Down, There And Back

Hollycombe is run by about 40 volunteers and those we met were unfailingly helpful, very enthusiastic, and willing to answer questions. They run several events through the year, such as craft fairs and model days, as well as Santa Specials at Christmas (fewer steam rides are available then and you need to book in advance).

FACT FILE

Address: Iron Hill, Liphook, Hampshire

Telephone: 01428 724900 and 01420 474740

Directions: By car use the A3 from London. Signposted and about 2 miles drive from A3, through Liphook village.

Public Transport: Train from Waterloo or clapham Junction to Liphook. Although Hollycombe is only about 1 mile from Liphook Station, it is an uphill walk along a lane with no footpath - not recommended with young children, so you would probably have to get a taxi from the station

Distance: 45 miles   **Travel time:** 1 hour

Opening: Sundays and Bank Holidays from Easter until mid October. Daily during much of the summer holidays. From about 1.00pm-6.00pm. Rides from 2.00pm

Prices: £4.50 adults, £3.50 children (under 2's free), for unlimited rides. Family ticket (2 adults, and 2 children £14.00)

Nappy changing facilities: No   **Restaurant facilities:** Cafe

High chairs: No   **Dogs:** No   **Pushchair-friendly:** ✓

Nearby: Dene Farm, a small farm with many animals for handling

Leighton Buzzard Railway

THIS SMALL SCALE, CHILD-SIZED LITTLE RAILWAY DIFFERS from other steam train rides in that most of the locomotives and carriage stock are rescued from industrial usage. Indeed, one of the best times to come is on one of the Industry Days (generally the second Sunday in the month), because then you can see specialised rolling stock carrying out the operations that it was designed for: peat wagons, sand transportation, munitions work, and forestry operations. Its all pretty grimy stuff – just what kids like. If your children get excited about road works then they will love seeing the huge 10RB diggers (giant mechanical excavators) doing their stuff there!

"Its all pretty grimy stuff – just what kids like!"

Originally a narrow gauge sand quarry railway, the line has been rescued and restored since its closure in the 1970's. Nowadays there are eleven steam engines in total owned by the line, of which three are working. On operational days you can do an hours return trip on the railway, but there are plenty of other things to keep you amused, so don't be snobbish; grab your 'sarnies' and make a day of it!

Start off at the tiny Page's Park station, which is located in a park on the outskirts of Leighton Buzzard. The station consists of a ticket office, small shop, buffet (no seats), portaloos, and, if you do the Santa Special in December, a welcoming coal fire. What it lacks in facilities is made up for by the friendly and enthusiastic staff. With two tree-lined platforms overlooking the narrow line, and a grassy bank to sit on, we happily watched the comings and goings of Peter Pan, Doll and Woto as they chugged in and out with the usual sighs, puffs and whistles you get on steam rides. The ride itself is in covered carriages, and goes rather unglamorously through back gardens to start with, which amused us, but of course the children didn't notice! You cross two level crossings, complete with a man with a red flag and several surprised-looking car drivers, before you get out into more open countryside, with fields, cows and hedgerows to admire.

Up, Down, There And Back

The terminus at Stonehenge Works is about two and a half miles down the line. You get off here whilst the engine does a 10-minute turnaround, however, it is worth stopping longer and getting the next train back, although do check in advance that there will be seating capacity on the return trip! Here at Stonehenge is the real grunge and grime associated with industrial railways. The workshop has expanded around a former stable building and now is an engineering base for the railway line – a workshop in the true sense of the word. There are always lots of little locos shunting backwards and forwards, a plethora of engine bits and pieces, engine cabins to scramble in and over, a visitor centre, and on the Industry Days, all sorts of equipment in working mode. ☛

The rolling stock has been rescued from all sorts of places - as far afield as India!

As at Page's Park station, there are plenty of knowledgeable and patient volunteers.

Back at Page's Park the park next to the station offers plenty of potential for a picnic and running around, and there is an excellent children's play area. For a real action-packed day out you could walk the half mile down to the Grand Union canal and watch the boats coming and going, or even take a trip yourself: the Leighton Lady (01525 384563) offers short trips on the canal and will give you a chance to see locks in operation too.

FACT FILE

Address: Leighton Buzzard Railway, Page's Park Station, Billington Road, Leighton Buzzard, Beds

Telephone: 01525 373888

Directions: Exit 11 on the M1, through Dunstable, taking the A5 towards Milton Keynes, and turn off into Leighton Buzzard. Follow the brown 'Narrow Gauge Railway' signs from Leighton Buzzard

Public transport: 45 minutes walk from Leighton Buzzard train station (trains from Euston)

Distance : 40 miles **Travel time:** 1 hour

Opening: Sundays, Easter, and Bank Holiday Mondays from mid March to Mid October, plus Wednesdays and some Thursdays in the summer. 11.00am-5.30pm

Prices: Adults £4.00, children £1.00, under-2's free

Nappy Changing facilities: No **Restaurant facilities**: No

High chairs: No **Dogs**: ✓ **Pushchair-friendly:** ✓

Nearby: Mead Open Farm (01525 851615), or Toddington Manor (01525 873566) for rare animals and vintage tractors

The Watercress Line

Up, Down, There And Back

THE STATION MASTER 'TOOT-TOOTS' HIS WHISTLE, the guard smartly waves a green flag, and with a gasp of steam and a belching cloud of billowing white smoke the huge locomotive heaves us out of the station. We're off!

If your children like the noise, bustle and excitement of real steam trains, then the Watercress Line is a must. It is a restored 10 mile stretch of railway running between Alton and Alresford in a beautiful rural part of Hampshire. There are currently three locomotives working – two steam, and one diesel – which are used to pull the carriages, as well as seven others in various stages of restoration. The four stations on the line; Alton, Medstead and Four Marks, Ropley, and Alresford, are all preserved and authentically recreate different periods in the railway's history, from the Twenties, to the late Fifties, with staff in appropriate uniforms, and period decoration and equipment. Our toddler loved it, especially being able to go inside the engine cab, and see all the shining knobs and dials!

For a good day out, start at Alton BR station (see how to get there in the fact file), and catch the train to Alresford in the morning. Rather incongruously, the platforms adjoin the BR commuter station. The journey takes about half an hour, with the train travelling through some lovely countryside as well as deep wooded cuttings. ☞

Alresford, when you get there, is a charming small town, with a lovely Georgian High Street, and several shops including antique and second-hand books (some open on Sundays). Have lunch outside at the Swan Hotel on the corner, or take a secret walk back to the station via the churchyard, catching a train back to Ropley, where you can picnic above the railway line, and watch the trains go by (marquee provided for wet weather). It is worth spending some time at Ropley in the afternoon, to see the engine shed with locomotives in the process of being restored – lots of grimy excitement here! There is also a children's play area there. You can stop at the other stations too: from Four Marks station there are two signposted woodland walks which are about a mile long. Great picnic potential here, but limited access with pushchairs.

"The train travels through some lovely countryside as well as deep wooded cuttings"

If you fancy a cream tea take the Countryman special back to Alton (you need to book this in advance). If you have time, you can have an enjoyable walk round Alton (pick up a walk description leaflet at the station), including feeding the ducks on Kings Pond, five minutes walk from the station.

The Watercress line runs on most Sundays of the year, Saturdays too from May to the end of October, and during the week at Easter and the summer months. Check the timetable in advance, as there are several different ones in operation. There are also lots of special events, such as a Teddy Bears Day, Thomas the Tank Engine Easter, Mother's Day (pre-booked teas!) and Fathers' Day (dad travels free) specials, a vintage bus day and Santa Specials at Christmas.

The Line is run by volunteers, and everyone we

encountered was very enthusiastic and helpful. There are buffet facilities on most trains and at the station restaurant in Alresford, as well as snacks at the station shops at Alton and Ropley. The shops sell the usual souvenirs and postcards. Nappy changing facilities are available at Alresford, elsewhere there are the usual station toilet facilities. The steps over the railway line at Alton were a bit awkward with a pushchair, and the trains themselves were bit narrow (single pushchairs okay, but double buggies beware!).

Up, Down, There And Back

FACT FILE

Address: Alresford Station, Hampshire

Telephone: 01962 733810/734200 Timetable: 01962 734866

Directions: By car take the A3 and A31 to Alton. Parking facilties at Alton and Alresford (pay and display)

Public Transport: There is a regular train service from Waterloo (stops at Clapham Junction and Wimbledon)

Distance: 45 miles   **Travel time:** 1hour 30 minutes

Opening: Sundays throughout the year, Saturdays from April to end October. Weekdays at Easter, half terms and during the summer. Trains every 45 minutes to one and a half hours, depending on season (check timetable in advance)

Prices: Adults £7.50, children £4.50. Under-5's free, except for Special Events, when 2 to 4 year-olds pay £2.50. Family £22.00

Nappy changing facilities: ✓   **Restaurant facilities:** ✓

High chairs: No   **Dogs:** ✓   **Pushchair-friendly:** ✓

Nearby: Alton and Alresford are both pleasant towns to walk around. The Devil's Punchbowl at Hindhead (20 miles away) is a great picnic and walks area

Bentley Wildfowl & Motor Museum

"There once was an ugly duckling..."

WITH ITS RATHER INCONGRUOUS COMBINATION OF vintage cars and waterfowl, Bentley is sure to appeal to most families. Set in an elegant country estate deep in the Sussex countryside it offers plenty for a good day out.

Depending on the weather, it is probably best to start with the birds. This gives you the chance to get rid of the bags of birdfood that your children will have persuaded you to buy at the entrance for 25p a bag. The birds are all 'housed' (or should it be 'nested'?) in a large series of enclosures, with wide pushchair-friendly paths. Some paths can be slightly muddy in places – especially after periods of wet weather. There is a lot of open water, and although most of it is fenced you will need to be a bit careful with toddlers. There is a choice of three routes around the enclosures – taking 30, 45 or 60 minutes respectively. Each route leads you through part of the collection: there are over 1000 swans, geese and ducks which can be readily seen and appreciated. Collect an identification chart at the entrance and ☞

You will see cars and birds of all different shapes and sizes

children will love spotting all the different varieties. Designed with close contact between birds and visitors in mind, there are plenty of opportunities for both adults and children to see the birds at close quarters, especially if you have food for them.

A new aviary is planned for 1995, up near the entrance, which will offer the chance to get close up to colourful, exotic birds, and the opportunity to shelter should it start to rain!

"Collect an identification chart and the children will love spotting all the different varieties of birds"

The motor museum should appeal to all car-freaks, large and small. The collection is very impressive. It is under cover and ranges from a 1960's bubble car (when did you last see one of those?), through gleaming Ferrari and Aston Martin sports numbers, to dinky-toy-like Vintage cars and bicycles. Unsurprisingly perhaps, children are not allowed to climb on the cars (well would you trust your precious antiques?), nevertheless it is a bit of a shame.

Outside again, the grounds have several further attractions. There is a woodland walk which takes about half an hour, and is resplendent in spring and summer with daffodils and bluebells. This may be passable in the summer with a pushchair, but when we went it was too muddy. A miniature steam train offers short rides for a small extra charge on all open Sundays, Bank Holiday Mondays and some other days during the school holidays. This has just been extended and from summer 1995 will take you up to the woods, with a short circuit in front of the woods, and a second station there. It runs about every five or ten minutes. There is also a nice adventure playground, not specifically designed for under-fives, but of course they loved it anyway.

Food and drinks are available in the small,

pleasant tea-room. Should you wish to sit outside this also has tables in the courtyard. The tea-room has a limited, but adequate menu of baked potatoes, sandwiches, and pasties, as well as teas and cakes. There is only one high chair. However, the extensive grassy grounds offer plenty of potential picnic spots.

The Great Outdoors

Next to the tea-room is a barn used as a small animal enclosure with pigs (plus piglets when we visited), sheep, rabbits and a chinchilla. The chinchilla kept himself to himself, but the other occupants provided yet another happy diversion.

FACT FILE

Address: Bentley Wildfowl and Motor Museum, Halland, E.Sussex

Telephone: 01825 840573

Directions: From the M25 take the A22 south to East Grinstead and on towards Eastbourne. Beyond Uckfield look for a brown sign off the A22, and after about 3 miles follow white signs to Bentley

Public Transport: None

Distance: 50 miles **Travel time:** 1 hour 30 minutes

Opening: Daily from mid March to the end of October 10.30am-4.30pm. Weekends only in February, March and November

Prices: Adults £3.80, children £2.20, under-4's free. Family ticket (2 adults and up to 4 children) £10.50. Reduced rates in winter

Nappy changing facilities: ✓ **Restaurant facilities:** ✓

High chairs: ✓(one) **Dogs:** No **Pushchair-friendly:** ✓

Nearby: Barkham Manor Vineyard offers wine tasting, vineyard trail, picnic site and tours of winery (01825 722103). For more vintage cars visit the Filching Manor Motor Museum, 15 miles further along the A22 at Jevington (01323 487838)

Blenheim Palace

MAKE THE TREK TO BLENHEIM PALACE WITH SMALL children when everyone is in the mood for a real day out. Despite it being a long journey from London, there are several attractions there to tempt you, and it is situated in beautiful Capability Brown parkland with a lake. With children the main interest is in the Pleasure Garden, where there are a walled games area, butterfly house, adventure playground and gardens, but there is also plenty of open parkland with great walks.

The Pleasure Garden is a 10-minute walk from the Palace itself. If you don't fancy the walk, there is a small single gauge railway that gets there in a few minutes, running from near the car park by the Palace. Trains run from 11.00am-5.30pm, departing every half an hour. If

The little train speeds you between the children's Pleasure Gardens and the Palace

you are aiming to go down at lunch time get to the station early, as a long queue forms at busy times. Similarly, the last trains back in the evening often fill up.

The highlights of the Pleasure Garden are within the walled games area. To enter this is £1.00 per adult, and you need to negotiate a tall, narrow turnstile with no separate pushchair entrance. Folding buggies can probably be passed over the top, but less portable pushchairs would need to be left at the entrance.

Inside the walled area is a large grassy play space, bisected by several paths and with a central fenced-off pond. The Marlborough Maze lies to the left, and is great fun. We weren't detered

by the notices saying buggies aren't permitted in the maze (as it contains two bridges with steps — these can easily be negotiated by experienced buggy users!). We solved the maze in about 20 minutes, with a great deal of cheating on the part of certain small people, who had a tendency to wriggle through gaps in the hedges!

Our children particularly enjoyed running around on the large plastic puzzle path, and hi-jacking the over-sized chess ☞

men and horses from the adjacent chess set. Chasing balls from the putting green was also very popular – although not with the people trying to play! Don't miss the model village. Although only one street long, it is crammed with tiny windows and courtyards for peering in. There is also a bouncy castle for two-to-five-year-olds, costing 50p per child. Outside of the walled garden the butterfly house is well worth a visit, although a bit difficult to negotiate with buggies. There are lots of brightly coloured flowers and butterflies.

"The Marlborough Maze is great fun"

The adventure playground is impressive, with a separate area for under-fives. Needless to say, few toddlers are satisfied with staying in their designated 'ghetto', and they tend to mingle with the older children on the rest of the equipment. This can be somewhat hair-raising!

You could easily spend a whole morning or afternoon down at the Pleasure Gardens. However, near the Palace are lovely views and easy walks on broad grassy paths – ideal for toddlers and pushchairs. There are two marked circuits: the Fisheries Cottage walk takes about half an hour, incorporating the cottage with its hens and wildfowl, and teeming trout in the lake inlet, whilst the other walk is longer (about an hours walk) and gives marvellous views of the park and Palace. Look out for sheep and lambs in the spring.

On the lake you can take a short motor cruise (included in the all-inclusive entrance price) or hire rowing boats for between £2.00 and £5.00 per hour, depending on the size of boat. Boats are not hired out in windy weather.

The Palace itself is magnificent, with Churchill memorabilia and a host of grand rooms with paintings and tapestries. Water terraces, and a formal Italian Garden complete the picture of opulence. Tours leave every ten minutes, and last one hour. Pushchairs are admitted.

The Great Outdoors

Eating facilities are good, with a spacious cafe in the Pleasure Gardens serving sandwiches, hot snacks, drinks and cakes. It has a terrace and lawn outside with benches and tables. A few high chairs are available. By the Palace there are two shops – one selling drinks and confectionery, and the other gifts and books. However, on a sunny day you could not do better than take a picnic into the park and admire the grandeur of the site whilst munching !

FACT FILE

Address: Blenheim Palace, Woodstock, Oxon

Telephone: 01993 811325 or 01993 811091 weekdays

Directions: Take the M40 beyond Oxford, and then follow the signs

Public Transport: None

Distance: 70 miles **Travel time:** 1 hour 45 minutes

Opening: Pleasure Garden and Palace from March to Ocober daily from 10.30am-4.45pm. The park is open all year 9.00am-4.45pm

Prices: All-inclusive ticket £7.00 adults, £3.50 children, under-5's free, family £19.00 (2 adults, 2 children). Park-only, £4.00 per car including all occupants

Nappy changing facilities: limited **Restaurant facilities:** ✓

High chairs: ✓ **Dogs:** ✓ on leads **Pushchair-friendly:** ✓

Nearby: Oxford, with its parks and river walks is always a pleasant place to visit.

Claremont Landscape Gardens

DESIGNED AND ESTABLISHED IN THE EIGHTEENTH century, and modified by Capability Brown, these gardens have recently been restored by the National Trust to form a peaceful and spacious area to stroll around within easy reach of London. For people with young children they offer an opportunity to wander in apparently natural surroundings of open countryside, but with paths for pushchairs and availability of other essential facilities (food, drink, loos, drink, loos and food!). Be warned, however, there is a large unfenced area of open water in the middle of the gardens, so you will need to keep an eye on toddlers.

> **"There are plenty of wide, grassy areas, ideal for resting, picnicing, or general running around"**

The car park and entrance kiosk are at the bottom of the gardens, near to the lake. You can follow the path round the lake, stopping to admire the many different kinds of wildfowl – Aylesbury, Mandarin, and Mallard ducks, black swans, and grebes, to name a few. As ever, the ducks are very amenable to being fed – a reliable toddler-diverting pastime, so bring some bread with you. The lake is also teeming with huge, glossy carp which glide just below the surface. They will actually come up and break the surface if you feed them (not recommended for those who didn't enjoy *Jaws*!).

A third of the way round the lake is a precarious looking pile of rocks, otherwise known as the grotto. This is great for those who like dripping, moss-infested caves and crannies. If you don't, move on quickly and you will come round to the other side of the lake, and have a good view of the island with its pavilion house (no access unfortunately), and the Ha-Ha (a grassy ditch to you and me). All around are huge, magnificent trees, and you can pick up a guide to them at the entrance kiosk, so that young children can have fun identifying them as you go round. Some trees date from as far back as the seventeenth and eighteenth centuries.

The Great
Outdoors

Once you are on the other side of the lake, the gardens open out more and there are plenty of wide, grassy areas, ideal for resting, picnicing, or general running around. The gardens continue up a hill behind the lake, and you can walk up through a camellia terrace, and along a lawned bowling ☞

Feeding the ducks and fishes may cause the only disturbance of the peace!

green, before stopping to admire the panorama from the amphitheatre at the top of the gardens. Return down to the lake via a path at the side of the amphitheatre.

The shop and cafe are small and clean, with two high chairs. There are some benches and tables outside too. The cafe is open 11.00am-5.00pm (3.30pm in winter) Tuesdays to Sundays and sells hot meals lunch-time, and teas, cakes, and drinks the rest of the time. The shop sells National Trust gifts, books and presents.

FACT FILE

Address: Claremont Landscape Gardens, Portsmouth Road, Esher, Surrey

Telephone: 01372 469421

Directions: Exit the A3 at the Esher turnoff. Go through Esher, and follow signs to the gardens, on the A307, just south of the town

Public Transport: Train to Esher, and about a 2 mile taxi ride from the station

Distance: 15 miles   **Travel time:** 30 minutes

Opening: All year, from 10.00am-7.00pm or dusk. Last admission half an hour before closing. Closed Christmas and New Year's Days

Prices: Adults £1.80 Monday to Saturday, £2.60 Sundays and Bank Holidays. Children half price, and under-5's free

Nappy changing facilities: ✓   **Restaurant facilities:** ✓

High chairs: ✓   **Dogs:** ✓ winter only

Pushchair-friendly: ✓

Nearby: Sandown Park Racecourse, and Esher town centre

Hatfield House

". . . but I have the heart and stomach of a king and of a king of England too. . ."

The Great Outdoors

A VISIT TO HATFIELD HOUSE PROVIDES YOU WITH A glimpse of a moment in history as well as offering a delightful haven of peace and tranquility just 20 miles from the hustle and bustle of Central London. The House's chief claim to historical fame is that it was here, sitting under an oak tree in the gardens, that Elizabeth I heard of her accession to the throne, and wandering through the extensive grounds it is easy to recapture that moment.

Hatfield House however has a great many pleasures to offer in addition to those of historical contemplation. The House itself is open to the public with hourly guided tours every day except Sunday. Buggies are allowed around the House but there is a certain amount of carrying to be done to get upstairs! The main house was built in Jacobean times by Robert Cecil and remains the family home of the Cecils. Only one wing of the old Palace in which Henry VIII housed his children now remains, adjacent to the main house. However, apart from the model soldiers exhibition

"Take a wander in the 'Wilderness Garden', a sea of daffodils in the spring and glorious colours in the autumn"

(3,000 toy soldiers in battle and display positions), the real delights for those with children are to be found outdoors.

Arriving with a fractious child on our hands we set aside all ideas of gentle strolls through the grounds and headed straight for the playground area, near the drive. This is very well laid-out with picnic tables provided, lots of room and a pretty setting surrounded by trees and countryside. ☛

There are glorious, extensive gardens to wander in whilst contemplating history

As well as swings and wooden play equipment, there is an adults' track to test whether you can get round without touching the ground: it has to be said that this was the favourite attraction in the playground for our daughter as she hopped from tree stump to tree stump!

As well as the playground there are a number of walks around the park, for example to the site of 'Queen Elizabeth's Oak'. The walks take you well

The Great
Outdoors

away from the house and again offer a different kind of experience. For these however you would be better off using backpacks rather than buggies because the ground is a bit rougher. The main gardens and extensive shrubbery next to the house are all however easily accessible for buggies (although we haven't been when the ground has been very wet).

The West Garden offers the main formal, cultivated gardens and is a toddler's delight as it consists of lots of little 'rooms', some with fountains in the centre, others with herbs, and often split by toddler height hedges. The presence of water and fountains does mean that you do need to keep an eye on the children before they decide to join the large fat fish in the ponds!

Alternatively, wander in the 'Wilderness Garden', a sea of daffodils in the spring and glorious colours in the autumn as the leaves begin to turn. This is a very peaceful special place with lots of room for children to roam in a safe and interesting environment. The ban ☛

on dogs gives it particular appeal (to non dog-owners!). We relaxed here whilst the children searched for twigs, all of us basking in the September sun.

As far as practicalities go, the stable area is the place to head for. There is a large, airy cafe with plenty of outdoor seating and a shop. It has lots of room for buggies (even double ones!) and a reasonably varied choice of food. There is a mother and baby room in the ladies loo: it is clean, has a chair for feeding and a bench for changing together with a sink.

FACT FILE

Address: Hatfield House, Hatfield, Herts

Telephone: 01707 262823

Directions: On the A1000 Great North Road, accessible from the A1(M). Signposted, and next to Hatfield train station

Public transport: Regular train service from Kings Cross to Hatfield

Distance: 20 miles **Travel time:** 45 minutes

Opening: From end of March to beginning of October (except Good Friday). Park, nature trail and play area from 10.30am-8.00pm , gardens 11.00am-6.00pm. House open every day except Monday

Prices: Park, gardens and exhibitions £2.80 adults, £2.10 children, under-5's free. All-inclusive £5.00 adults, £3.20 children

Nappy changing facilities: ✓   **Restaurant facilities:** ✓

High chairs: ✓   **Dogs:** No

Pushchair-friendly: ✓

Nearby: Knebworth House (see page 110)

Penshurst Place

LOOKING FOR A HAVEN OF TRANQUILLITY (FOR adults), with plenty to offer children as a treat? Set in an intimate patchwork of small fields, mature hedgerows and deciduous trees, Penshurst Place is a small stately home, surrounded by a myriad of interconnecting gardens and orchards.

From the car park follow the gravel path up towards the house, and through mellow sandstone-turreted courtyards to the gardens, which radiate out in front. With a mixture of formal gardens, shady orchards (replete with polished apples when we were there), open grassy spaces and wide flower borders, great fun can be had exploring all the different nooks and crannies. Boo! We had lots of hide and seek games behind the tall box yew hedges. Beware though, there are a few deep ponds (with goldfish lurking) – so try and keep up with your little Captain Cooks! When we went it was very peaceful everywhere, but nobody seemed to mind how much noise the children made!

The medieval splendour of the house is probably left for adults to enjoy. It costs a bit more (adult price for house and grounds is £4.95), and we didn't ☞

Peaceful and intimate gardens with lots to divert the kids

bother, although we did peek inside the magnificent 650-year-old Baronial Hall. However, we'd recommend a visit to the toy museum, located in a small annexe. There is no extra charge, and it makes a fascinating diversion. Our little girl loved the old-fashioned dolls and teddy bears dressed in lace finery, although with lots of 'Do Not Touch' notices our two-year-old son was somewhat of a liability! The highlight of the museum for both of them was the Drinking Bear – so take some 2p pieces with you. Restaurant and tea-rooms are nearby.

"Don't miss the magnificent adventure playground, it's one of the best"

Don't miss the magnificent adventure playground, one of the best I've seen. It has activities for all ages of children – sandpit, slides, balancing poles and swings for the younger ones, and awe-inspiring high level runs and commando-style assault courses for older athletes. The tunnel maze mound looks like it should be for older children, but our little ones soon proved us wrong – you may find keeping all the exits covered when it is time to leave quite a challenge (unless you fancy crawling inside a muddy three foot high tunnel on your knees. . .). Set in a lovely sunny grassy bowl, with lots of picnic tables and benches, the playground is a great place for kids to let off steam whilst you recuperate. The adjoining barn has a picnic area upstairs, agricultural and countryside exhibits, and a small gift and tuck shop where you can pick up colouring cards, leaflets for the nature trail and things to eat.

The nature trail is rewarding. It is a mile-long walk through woods and past fishponds. It takes between 30 minutes and an hour to complete, depending on how often you stop to admire all the fauns and flora along the way. It is manageable with pushchairs in dry weather, but too muddy after a wet spell.

If you need an incentive to visit, several special events are held in the grounds during the season – classic car rallies, craft days and hot-air balloon festivals all offer good child-appeal. There are also falconry displays held on Saturdays in July and August when you can meet and handle owls, falcons and hawks.

The Great Outdoors

If you like cream teas, the village of Penshurst has two tearooms, whilst there are several good pubs offering tasty brews in the area for alternative lunch stops.

FACT FILE

Address: Penshurst Place, Penshurst, Tonbridge, Kent
....
Telephone: 01892 870307
....
Directions: M25 junction 5. Then A21 south, leaving at the Tonbridge North exit. Then follow the brown signs
....
Public transport: Tonbridge train station (trains from Victoria) is six miles away, with plenty of taxis available
....
Distance: 45 miles   **Travel time:** One hour 15 minutes
....
Opening: Daily from end March to end September. Saturdays and Sundays in March and October. 11.00am-6.00pm.
....
Prices: Grounds only (including toy museum) £3.50 adults, £2.25 children. Under 5's free. Family ticket to house and grounds £13.00
....
Nappy changing facilities: ✓   **Restaurant facilities:** ✓
....
High chairs: ✓ (one)   **Dogs:** No
....
Pushchair-friendly: ✓
....
Nearby: Hollanden Rare Animals Farm Park (01732 833858), Chiddingstone and Hever Castles

The Whitbread Hop Farm

AS YOU APPROACH THE HOP FARM YOU ARE REWARDED with a spectacular and unmistakable view of twenty huge oast houses silhouetted against the sky. In lovely countryside, and with several attractions for young children, the farm is well worth a visit, especially in the summer, or when the weather is not too bad.

Once you have negotiated the reception area and shop (beware – the sweets are displayed in toddler-height pick and mix boxes, ideal for little fingers to explore whilst you are preoccupied paying the entrance fee!), you come out into a large grassy area, with gravelled paths leading between the oast houses, restaurant block and stable block. Start with the stable block, which is home to the enormous Shire horses, used in times past to deliver beer around London. Now these magnificent beasts are used for displays and processions, and you can see demonstrations of grooming, harnessing and driving. Watch them elegantly lifting their huge feathered feet and tossing their manes as they trot around the farm. You can also go on short trailer rides, pulled by two horses, and look at the exhibits of old-fashioned drays. Unfortunately, children aren't allow to climb on these, which is a pity!

> **"The stable block is home to the enormous Shire horses, used in times past to deliver beer around London"**

Across from the stables is an aviary, where you can get a good close up look at several different kinds of birds of prey. Amazingly, owls and the like will sit quite motionless whilst children shriek and cavort a few feet away. The highlight of this part of the farm is the flying displays, when owls are flown by a falconer. Much excitement can be

had by even very young children, who can have a go wearing the falconer's glove and letting the owl fly onto their outstretched arm. Displays are usually given mornings and afternoons, weather permitting, but the times do vary depending on which birds are being flown.

Despite their immense size the Shire horses are surprisingly approachable

The farm is host to an animal village, featuring a good range of small furry beasts – rabbits, guinea pigs, miniature ponies, goats and the like. These are nicely kept in toddler-height pens, and provide the usual amusement for young children. Handling and touching opportunities are a bit limited though.

There is an adventure playground set a short walk away from the stables. This was quiet when we ☞

visited it, and our children had a great time. However, in more crowded periods it could be a bit boisterous, as there is no separate play area for the under-fives. The grounds are lovely, with plenty of picnic spots. If it rains the hop museum inside some of the oast houses will amuse you for a little while, with its re-creation of the sights and sounds of the hop-picking heyday some 50 years ago.

The restaurant sells a good variety of hot meals, drinks, cakes, sandwiches and snacks. It is spacious, with plenty of high chairs, but not all had straps.

FACT FILE

Address: The Whitbread Hop Farm, Beltring, Paddock Wood, Kent

Telephone: 01622 872068

Directions: Take the M20, and exit at Junction 4 for Paddock Wood. Go on in towards Paddock Wood, following the signposts to the farm

Public Transport: Train to Paddock Wood from Charing Cross (trains on the hour and half hour, taking 50 minutes), and taxi from the station

Distance: 40 miles   **Travel time:** 1 hour 30 minutes

Opening: Open all year, excluding Christmas, Boxing and New Years Days. Open 10.00am-6.00pm in the summer and 10.00am-4.00pm in the winter. Last admission one hour before closing

Prices: £4.95 adults, £3.00 children, under-5's free

Nappy changing facilities: ✓   **Restaurant facilities:** ✓

High chairs: ✓   **Dogs:** ✓ on leads

Pushchair-friendly: ✓

Nearby: Badsell Park Farm is about five miles away (see page 19)

Wisley Royal Horticultural Society Gardens

The Great Outdoors

"With silver bells and cockle shells and pretty maids all in a row"

WISLEY GARDENS ARE A TREAT — A SHORT DRIVE down the A3, plenty of room for children to safely run about, and gorgeous gardens to admire at the same time. Although really an adult outing, children are very well accommodated for. However, be warned, if you are despairing over the state of your own tangled weed-bed, the various displays of excellence will depress you even more!

The gardens are open all year, and offer something in all seasons. They are large enough to get away from everyone else if you want, and are organised into over twenty different areas. There are heaps of wonderful lawns for running/crawling on, wide paths ideal for pushchairs (follow the wheelchair route to avoid any steps at all), and plenty of toddler-height walls for balancing practice. If you go there a lot (and it is quite possible to without getting bored), you will probably latch on to your own favourite places. Our favourites include the fruit fields and gardens, which display a huge variety of tree and soft fruits in all sorts of forms, from those

"It might be better to leave your credit cards at home if you have a weakness for plant sales!"

suited to small gardens to awe-inspiring fan-trained trees. In case the fruit are proving too tempting to eager little fingers, it is worth remembering that all fruit in season is sold next to the car park from 1.00pm-4.00pm every day. The Rock Garden, with its myriad of little paths and steps is also a ☞

favourite, along with the herbaceous borders and rose gardens (dazzling in summer) and the colourful trees and heather gardens in the Pinetum and Howard's Field. Older children may enjoy following the Children's Trail – pick up a leaflet at the entrance.

Should your children tire of running in the gardens there is a pond and a lake across from the restaurant, which have ducks and huge goldfish lurking in the depths.

Although not really a wet-weather day out there is a large greenhouse, with hot, warm and cool plant displays, which is ideal to duck into if you find you need shelter!

Other facilities at Wisley are very good. There is a large cafe, with ample space, plenty of high chairs (though none with straps), and a terrace with tables overlooking a larged lawned area – ideal in the

Increase your gardening knowledge in the extensive gardens which are easily navigated by kids and pushchairs

summer. Hot and cold food, drinks, cakes and snacks are available in the cafe, and there is also a more formal restaurant next door. You are not permitted to picnic in the gardens, but there is a picnic area outside, near to the car park.

The Great
Outdoors

The shop next to the entrance is large and sells a variety of gifts, books and stationery. There is also a very good plant shop for shrubs, trees, bedding plants, seeds etc – take notes as you go around the gardens, and you can buy all the plants in the shop! (Better to leave your credit cards at home?)

FACT FILE

Address: Royal Horticultural Society Gardens, Wisley, Woking, Surrey

Telephone: 01483 224234

Directions: Take A3 from London, or M25 (exit 10), follow the signs just beyond the A3 and M25 intersection

Public Transport: Train from Waterloo or Clapham Junction to West Byfleet or Woking, and then a two or three mile taxi ride. Alternatively London Country Bus number 415 from Victoria

Distance: 20 miles   **Travel time:** 30 minutes

Opening: 10.00am-7.00pm in summer, 10.00am-sunset in winter. Monday to Saturday throughout the year (except Christmas Day). Open only to RHS members on Sundays

Prices: £4.70 adults, £1.75 children. Under-6's free. Free to RHS members

Nappy changing facilities: ✓   **Restaurant facilities:** ✓

High chairs: ✓   **Dogs:** No   **Pushchair-friendly:** ✓

Nearby: The Angel Pub at Pyrford Lock on the River Wey offers pub food and welcomes families. See also Lockwood Donkey Sanctuary (page 38) and Loseley Park Farm (page 41)

Look! Look! Look !
Exhibitions And Things To See

Bekonscot Model Village

STEP BACK INTO THE WORLD OF 1930'S AGATHA Christie England and visit this charming and intricate model village. The tidy world-in-miniature displayed has efficient-seeming trains chugging about, cars with running boards, village corner shops and pubs, and wholesome, cheerful model people. The detail is superb, with a lot of humorous touches for adults (someone obviously had fun

With a wealth of tiny features and detail the model village fascinates adults and children alike

with the pub and shop names!), whilst there are a wealth of tiny features to amuse and fascinate children. Thoughtfully provided with picnic spots and an adventure playground too, Bekonscot makes an easy, fun day out with something for everyone. However, it is very popular in August, and can get crowded, whilst in the summer term there are often school visits in the morning, so it is probably best to time your arrival for lunch or just afterwards.

Look!
Look!
Look!

The village is set in one and a half acres of garden, and has over 160 buildings. A microcosm of idealised rural and village life is represented: shops (even a 1950's Marks & Spencer!), churches, schools, castles, with a zoo, fishing harbour, fairground and racecourse, to name just a few of the features. A sinewy, narrow path snakes in and out and up and down through the village and surrounding 'countryside', providing good variety and the chance the see all the detail well, often at eye-level.

It took us about an hour to go all the way round once.

You have to follow the path and set route through, and with limited passing places, this means it may get frustrating at busy times. However, you can go round and round as many times as you like! The path was easily passable with our single buggy, but a double buggy would get stuck. You can use the (single) buggies ☞

provided at the entrance if your own pushchair is too wide.

A model railway with five trains busily runs around covering more or less the whole site. With several stations, lots of tunnels, viaducts and bridges, trains seem to keep popping-up everywhere, and offer great scope for distraction at any time. You can even see inside the life-sized signal box, where the signalman controls the points and signals with levers, just like a real railway.

"The model village has over one hundred and sixty buildings"

No village would be complete without its babbling brook and, true to life, you will find one at Bekonscot. The little stream merrily runs through part of the village, passing over a water wheel attached to a mill, and down over a waterfall into the 'sea', which, complete with pier, fishing harbour and lighthouse, is one of the most attractive features of the village. If you wonder what the wires running over the water are for, it is to discourage herons landing to make a meal of the huge carp lurking underwater!

The garden that the village is set in is wonderfully designed and maintained, and has lots of lovely miniature trees and shrubs, as well as a host of rockery plants and flowers. In the spring and summer the gardens are beautiful. There are full-sized trees too, with benches around, which provide welcome resting points in the shade for the footsore.

The village is well set up for picnics, with lots of picnic tables and benches in one corner. The refreshment kiosk is at the far end of the village, selling pizzas, burgers and hot dogs, as well as sandwiches, snacks, ices and teas. You can sit on tables and benches at the picnic area near the kiosk, but there is no inside seating there. However, there is a greenhouse near the main entrance with tables and seats, and you can sit there in wet or cold weather. As an alternative, Jung's cafe in Beaconsfield village (5 minutes walk from Bekonscot) serves hot meals and has high chairs and pleasant staff.

Look!
Look!
Look!

The adventure playground has good slides and climbing castles, with seating for parents and guardians. Its not huge, and may be hectic sometimes!

A shop at the entrance, located in an old railway carriage, has a small range of small toys and gifts.

FACT FILE

Address: Bekonscot Model Village, Warwick Road, Beaconsfield, Bucks

Telephone: 01494 672919

Directions: Take the M40, leaving at Junction 2, signposted for Beaconsfield and The Model Village. Follow the Model Village signs. Bekonscot is off a side road behind Waitrose in Beaconsfield New village

Public Transport: Train from Marylebone to Beaconsfield (8-10 minutes walk)

Distance : 30 miles   **Travel time:** 50 minutes to 1 hour

Opening: Every day 10.00am-5.00pm. From mid-February until the end of October

Prices: £3.00 adults, £1.50 children. Under-3's free

Nappy changing facilities: ✓   **Restaurant facilities:** Limited

High chairs: No   **Dogs:** No   **Pushchair-friendly:** ✓

Nearby: A spooky visit to Hell Fire Caverns in West Wycombe Caves (01494 33739), or try Burnham Beeches, a lovely picnic spot nearby (follow signs to Wooburn Green)

Brighton Sea Life Centre

BRIGHTON IS ALWAYS A FUN PLACE TO VISIT WITH young children – not only is there the sea (albeit with a pebbly beach), and a grand pier to stroll along, but also you can wander through the maze of little shops in the Lanes area (behind the sea front), or have a picnic and cup of tea in the delightful park next to the Pavilion buildings. The Sea Life Centre, next to the pier, is completely indoors and means that Brighton is still worth a day trip even in wet or cold weather.

If you and your children are not completely fazed by practically rubbing noses with a shark or tickling a sting-ray, then you will have a wonderful time at the Centre. You start by walking through a series of sea and freshwater aquariums in the elegantly restored Victorian display area. Huge fish glide literally inches away in floor to ceiling tanks,

"For the brave (or foolhardy) there are instructions given on how to stroke the sting-rays"

which are subtly-lit and ingeniously modelled to re-create underwater scenes. Wrecks, sunken treasure and ominous caverns abound. The size of the tanks and the well-provided viewing platforms means that children (even those in pushchairs) can get a really good view.

These displays open out into a wider area, where a sandy sea-bed has been re-created on one side, and an old harbour the other. The sandy sea-bed is teeming with graceful sting-rays, which rear up out of the water almost as if they are saying hello. For the brave (or foolhardy) there are instructions given on how to stroke the rays. Apparently these two-to-three-foot long creatures are very gentle and do not sting unless you tread on them. Note that over-enthusiastic little hands would not be able to reach the rays on their own – if you wanted your children to touch the rays you would have to lift them over the guard rail. The old harbour is full of creaking boards and sounds of seagulls, with plenty of huge crabs dancing over the sea-bed. Feed the creatures in these open tanks, if you dare! (food on sale at the entrance for 50p).

Look!
Look!
Look!

Walk on through more tanks displaying deep-water creatures, such as octopus and lobsters. Some of these tanks have special viewing 'bubbles', which enable you to feel that you are in the water with the beastees! The *piece de resistance*, though, is the underwater tunnel, which offers superb close up views of British sharks, more sting-rays, and conger eels. We were there at feeding time, which was fascinating, but not for the squeamish! Suffice to say, much enjoyment was had by all as these mysterious animals glided and cavorted above our heads.

The Centre is well set up with other facilities for young children. There is a small soft play area, next to the sandy sea-shore display, a video unit, and plenty of excellent audio-visual displays. ☞

Even the smallest visitors can get wonderfully close up to all the creatures

Sammy's cafe sells a variety of hot meals and snacks, and has a limited number of high chairs. It caters for birthday parties if you book in advance. There is also a shop which sells a good variety of fishy style gifts, toys and sweets. Feeding of the denizens of the deep takes place twice a day, although it is not always the creatures in the tunnel.

The Centre is easily accessible with a pushchair. Don't be deterred at the entrance by the long flight of steps down, there is a side disabled entrance leading off the seafront, with no steps to negotiate at all!

FACT FILE

Address: Brighton Sea Life Centre, Marine Parade, Brighton

Telephone: 01273 604233 (24 hour information line). Bookings 01273 604234

Directions: Take the M23, and A23 straight to Brighton and head for the sea front

Public Transport: Frequent train services from Victoria station. Brighton station is about 15 minutes walk from the Centre

Distance: 50 miles **Travel time:** 1 hour to 1 hour 30 minutes

Opening: 10.00am-5.00pm every day, except Christmas. Later in summer

Prices: Adults £4.50, children £3.25 Under-4's free

Nappy changing facilities: ✓ **Restaurant facilities:** ✓

High chairs: ✓ **Dogs:** No **Pushchair-friendly:** ✓

Nearby: Brighton Toy and Model Museum, next to the train station, is open daily. During the summer the Volks electric railway on the sea front offers short rides along the coast. There are plenty of shops, parks and restaurants in the town, including lots of fish and chip shops!

Didcot Railway Centre
"Aye, man and boy, and my father too, and his father before him . . ."

Look!
Look!
Look!

GRAB YOUR THERMOS, DON YOUR ANORAK AND SET OFF for a day in homage to God's Wonderful Railway (GWR or the Great Western Railway) at Didcot. Here you can marvel at some of the heaviest and strongest steam engines ever built. Move over Thomas – here comes the 3288! If you think you've had enough of steam engine romanticism, think again – this one is not to be missed.

Didcot was a centre of operations for the Great Western Railway from its heyday at the early part of this century through to its closure in the mid 1960's. Now a museum of those golden days of steam, it has one of the largest and most impressive collections of steam engines, carriages and steam memorabilia in the country. The collection is held on track and sidings alongside Didcot railway station, and is lovingly cared for by members of the Great Western Railway Society, from whose 8,000 members come volunteers who will readily strip down an engine at the drop of a spanner, or regale visitors with tales from the glory days.

Beware: the heady mix of enthusiasm and reverence at Didcot are quite catching!

The museum makes a great day out with young children. There are about 20 to 25 actual steam engines – including the beasts Britannia and the Duke of Gloucester, the TGV's of their day. Many are operational and can be seen in action on steam days (generally first and last weekends of the month, and Wednesdays in the summer, but do check in ☛

advance). The sheer scale of these mighty engines – the driving wheels stand taller than a man – creates an awe-inspiring sense of power, which sets Didcot apart from many of the more usual steam enthusiasts' railways. There is heaps to see and do: we walked right alongside the tracks with the great beasts towering above, enjoyed clambering up into the engine driver's compartments in the engine sheds, and relaxed in 1930's carriages pulled short distances down the line by puffing, whistling steam trains. There was plenty of activity with lots of shunting backwards and forwards, and engines and carriages being moved to and fro – we just missed seeing the huge turntable in operation, but were assured that it is so finely balanced that it only takes two or three men to turn an engine (at a maximum weight of 175 tons this seemed an incredible feat!). It is safe enough for young children, but if you are nervous take reins for toddlers.

Apart from the engine sheds the site has many other railway relics. We liked the 24-lever 1898 Radstock North signal box (winner of the 1989 Best Restored Signal Box Award – how many signal boxes are restored each year, we asked ourselves?), which you can sometimes see in operation, and the carriage shed full of restored, partly restored and just plain salvaged carriages. The Relics Museum is an indoor collection of bits and pieces, including a re-created station master's office, railway toys and model trains (attracting several fascinated children to jostle for position on the kids viewing platform).

"The sheer scale of these mighty engines creates an awe-inspiring sense of power"

There is a typical station restaurant with formica-topped tables, smelling of chips and with the requisite steamy windows and mugs of strong tea. There is also a grassy picnic area with tables and benches, and two shops – the bookshop with a mix of Thomas The Tank toys and real train-spotters equipment, and the relics shop, selling railway magazine archive material.

Special events are held throughout the year: Santa Specials, Easter Egg hunts, Teddy Bears' picnic, and Thomas the Tank Engine days. Although not really a wet weather day out, do try a winter trip as the steam shows up better in colder weather.

Look!
Look!
Look!

Didcot will make a train-spotter of you. We restrained ourselves from buying the tapes of engine steam sounds, but our daughter is still saving for the £1,500 hire fee for the 3288 freight engine – anyone got a few miles of railway track we can borrow?

FACT FILE

Address: Didcot Railway Centre, Didcot, Oxfordshire

....

Telephone: 01235 817200

....

Directions: Signposted from junction 13 of the M4 motorway

....

Public transport: Regular fast trains from Paddington to Didcot Parkway (about 1 hours trip)

....

Distance: 53 miles   **Travel time:** 1 hour 30 minutes

....

Opening: Saturdays and Sundays all year, daily from April to end of September, 11.00am-5.00pm or dusk. Check timetable for steaming days

....

Prices: £4.50 adults, £3.00 children, under-5's free. Family ticket £13.00

....

Nappy changing facilities: ✓   **Restaurant facilities:** ✓

....

High chairs: No   **Dogs:** ✓ on leads

....

Pushchair-friendly: ✓

....

Nearby: Childe Beale wildlife park (01734 845172)

Gatwick Airport
& Zoo

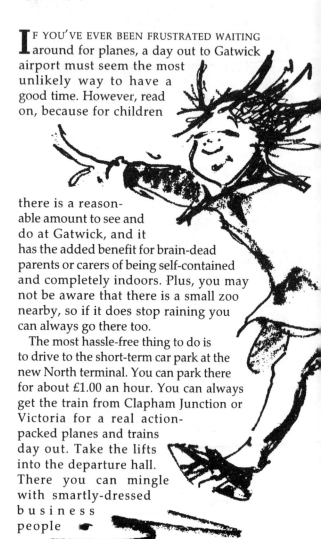

IF YOU'VE EVER BEEN FRUSTRATED WAITING around for planes, a day out to Gatwick airport must seem the most unlikely way to have a good time. However, read on, because for children

there is a reasonable amount to see and do at Gatwick, and it has the added benefit for brain-dead parents or carers of being self-contained and completely indoors. Plus, you may not be aware that there is a small zoo nearby, so if it does stop raining you can always go there too.

The most hassle-free thing to do is to drive to the short-term car park at the new North terminal. You can park there for about £1.00 an hour. You can always get the train from Clapham Junction or Victoria for a real action-packed planes and trains day out. Take the lifts into the departure hall. There you can mingle with smartly-dressed b u s i n e s s people

Children will love seeing the planes close-up, instead of just as streaks in the sky (remember that?), exotic travellers from far-flung (warm, no doubt) places, and other people like yourself with nothing better to do. Inside the departure hall there are plenty of shops, notably Boots, the Body Shop, and WH Smiths, and a wealth of restaurants and snack bars. For older children there is even a flight simulator.

> "From the spectator viewing gallery you can watch, hear and smell the huge jets launch themselves skywards"

Once you get bored, take the transit train to the South terminal. This short aerial train ride offers views of the airport from large picture windows. In the South terminal there is one of those moving 'traveolator' things, which provide a fair degree of amusement for toddlers (keep hold of children, though, as the traveolator could be dangerous). More shops, business people, and travellers can be found inside the South terminal. At the arrivals end of the terminal you can take the lifts to the top floor, and the spectator viewing gallery. This is on the roof, and offers a wonderful view of the main runway, as well as one of the main loading and parking bays. You can watch, hear and smell the huge jets manoeuvre out and taxi onto the runway, forming orderly queues, before launching themselves skywards, and disappearing. Alternatively, speculate on where all the landing planes, belly-flopping onto the runway, have flown in from and see how many different airline liveries you can spot. The spectator shop, recently re-furbished, sells cards, model planes, calendars and videos, as well as information for plane freaks.

If you have time and energy, you could visit Charlwood Zoo, which is about 3 miles from the airport. Although not really an excursion in its own right, it makes a valuable extra diversion if you are in the vicinity. To get there drive past the North terminal, and follow signs to Crawley and Redhill. The zoo is signposted with brown cockatoo signs from just beyond the airport. It is a small zoo and aviary, manageable in about an hour to an hour and a half. You can buy food for the animals at the entrance (35p a cup), and watch the monkeys playing on a moated island with tree ropes, swings and a house. There is a small adventure playground (which can be a bit muddy), and a picnic area, as well as a little cafe selling sandwiches and other light refreshments.

Look!
Look!
Look!

FACT FILE

Address: Gatwick Airport, Crawley, Surrey and Gatwick Zoo, Russ Hill, Charlwood, Surrey
....
Telephone: Airport 01293 535353, Zoo 01293 862312
....
Directions: M23 London to Brighton road. Take the Gatwick airport exit and follow signs
....
Public Transport: Train to Gatwick airport from Victoria or Clapham Junction (comes into the South terminal). Open-top buses numbers 88 and 439 go to Zoo from airport weekends and Bank Holidays.
....
Distance: 30 miles **Travel time:** 1 hour
....
Opening: Airport, all times. Spectator viewing 8.00am-7.00pm in the summer, and 9.00am-4.00pm in the winter. The Zoo opens every day March to October, 10.30am-5.00pm, and weekends and school holidays November to February, 10.30am to dusk
....
Prices: Airport spectator area 60p adults, 30p children, under-5's free. Zoo £3.75 adults, £2.75 children, under-2's free
....
Nappy changing facilities: ✓ (not Zoo) **Restaurant facilities:** ✓
....
High chairs: ✓ (not Zoo) **Dogs:** ✓ (not Zoo) **Pushchair-friendly:** ✓
....
Nearby: The North Downs, around Leith Hill, has lovely walks

Kempton Park Races

"I bet my money on a bobtailed nag, doo-da, doo-da"

AND THEY'RE OFF! AND SO WERE WE FOR A DAY AT THE races. Horse-racing is probably one of the few major spectator sports that are compatible with young children. For all the hustle and bustle, there is a friendly atmosphere and you will find that many people bring children. At Kempton Park they have recognised this and invested in a creche, so that little ones can take a break from the afternoon's entertainment if they want.

Access could not be much easier – one popular way is to come by car with a jolly good picnic, and park in the middle of the course – wandering to the rails for each race as it comes along. There is also a dedicated railway station right by the course, with

frequent services from Waterloo on race days.

Look!
Look!
Look!

Once on the course, mingle with the crowds in the Silver Ring enclosure. Between races there is an ever-changing kaleidoscope of people from all walks of life; bookies shaving their odds (get your children to research the best odds), 'tic-tac men' signalling the odds to unseen watchers, and horses warming up on the course. Or go round the back of the stands to the paddock, where the horses begin their pre-race preparation. Usually you can get close enough for a really good look at these magnificent beasts, all gleaming coats and slender, muscled legs.

Try to place a bet on each race – it makes it much more fun. You will find that bookies in the Silver Ring enclosure expect a minimum bet of £2.00. No need to spend the morning in the Public Library comparing the odds and boning up on the colours of the jockeys' silks, however. Our experience is that any daily newspaper carries extensive ☛

It's hard not to yell and cry screams of encouragement as the horses thunder up the course

discussion of the relative merits of the main contenders, enabling you to carry on a seemingly knowledgeable conversation before making your choice. You can also buy programmes on course which carry quite a lot of information, if you want to really get into it. Children love to get involved, they can see the horses in the paddock and choose the one they like best, or choose a favourite number or colour.

> **"Between races there is an ever-changing kaleidoscope of people from all walks of life"**

When you have exhausted the fun to be had in the Silver Ring, there is often further entertainment to be had on the racecourse. Sponsors often arrange exhibitions and demonstrations.

If your children are very young or simply get tired and want a break there is a free creche. It is located in the Silver Ring enclosure, behind the main stand. It is quite simple, but adequately equipped, and there are plenty of enthusiastic and willing helpers. It is rather small though, with a capacity of about 20 children. You can leave children from 0 to eight years old, and for up to an hour on busy days, longer when it is quiet. It is probably a good idea to ensure you get there early if you definitely want to leave your children there for a period.

Other facilities for children are fairly limited. Toilets are basic, and do not boast nappy changing facilities, though you can change a nappy in the creche, even if there is not room to leave your child. The eating and drinking places are take-away bars and caravans. Great for slumming it with chips and tomato ketchup, but be warned that there are no high chairs, sit-down cafes or picnics in the Silver Ring enclosure.

Excitement always runs high for the King George VI Stakes on Boxing Day (you know, the one that Desert Orchid always used to win) and joining the big crowd there to eat your turkey sandwiches makes a great change. There are meetings throughout the year of course; a warm sunny day can be wonderful for a relaxed picnic. At the height of summer, there are evening meetings (some with fireworks), with the last race at about 9.00pm. The creche is available for these evening meetings too.

Look!
Look!
Look!

One final tip – leave before the last race if you have travelled by car. The car parks exit onto the narrow roads around Sunbury which soon jam with the sudden heavy traffic flow at the end of the day's racing. It can take over an hour to get out of the car

FACT FILE

Address: Kempton Park Racecourse, Sunbury on Thames, Middlesex

Telephone: 01932 782292

Directions: A316 from west London to Sunbury, then follow the signs for the racecourse. Kempton Park is just off the A308.

Public Transport: Train from Waterloo on race days

Distance: 20 miles   **Travel time:** 45 minutes

Opening: 1 or 2 meetings most months, more in the summer when there are evening meetings too. Telephone in advance to see which days. Most afternoon meetings start at 2.00pm, and evening ones at 6.00pm. You can usually go in about an hour before the first race

Prices: Silver Ring £5.00-£7.00, grandstand £12.00-£15.00, depending on event. Children free

Nappy changing facilities: None, except in creche

Restaurant facilities: Takeaway only

High chairs: No   **Dogs:** No   **Pushchair-friendly:** ✓

Nearby: Bushy Park and Hampton Court

Knebworth House

IF KNEBWORTH HOUSE MEANS ROCK CONCERTS AND distant memories of child-free days, think again! It actually offers a comprehensive day out for the family, with a magnificent stately home, park and gardens complemented by a children's adventure area at Fort Knebworth.

Our first impressions at Knebworth were dispiriting. Just as we drew into the car park, the heavens opened and the wind started blowing furiously so we made a dash for the cafe. This is a 16th century Tithe barn in the stable block outbuildings and whilst the building is very attractive, the cafe itself was somewhat dark and had an unloved air. It is doubtless more welcoming on a better day – in any case you can always sit outside if you want. However, after this rather disappointing beginning things got better and better.

"Knebworth is a wonderfully impressive house complete with Gothic battlements and heraldic beasts"

Knebworth House is the home of the Lytton family and it retains a real sense of being a private residence. It is a wonderfully impressive large house complete with Gothic battlements and heraldic beasts. The interior is sufficiently small and compact to be able to dash around with children, peer at a few family photographs, take in a little history and marvel (or grimace) at the armoury, without hitting a boredom threshold! In our case it was quite the reverse as the rooms are only roped off and buggies have to be left in the entrance hall, so it was more a case of persuading curious toddlers that all those interesting looking objects really weren't a wonderful new set of toys presented just for their amusement! The attendants in the house were very friendly, and knowledgeable, and not fazed (or they didn't show it) by the potential disruption.

Several special events are planned for 1995: for those with children the most popular would probably be the re-enaction of an American Civil War battle (16th and 17th April), and the MG or Morris car owners' club rallies during the summer.

The gardens were a delight for us and a large tree with branches descending to the ground provided our daughter with at least half an hour's entertainment as she learnt the finer points of tree climbing. Each of us had the opportunity to explore some of the borders and further reaches of the garden alone. The park is delightfully extensive, with herds of Red and Sika deer, and is ideal for walks and picnics.

Fort Knebworth, which is an enclosed children's adventure playground, is about half a mile away near the park entrance. It is clearly popular with local families and there were a couple of children's birthday parties taking place with the adults sitting back and enjoying the picnic whilst the kids were off playing. This said, it is quite exposed in bad weather and the only covered picnic area is a bit like a ☞

Look!
Look!
Look!

For us, the house and gardens were the highlights, whilst for our daughter Fort Knebworth was the place to be

bandstand and hence open to the elements! However, the playground itself is extensive and offers something for most age groups.

There are also a couple of extras which make it that little bit special as a place to take the children. One is the Astroglide – a giant slide which you go down sitting on special mats with a fast lane for the real thrill seekers! And as well as the bouncy castle and a little miniature railway, there are other activity features for children and adults which will keep them occupied for ages.

FACT FILE

Address: Knebworth House, Knebworth, Herts

Telephone: 0438 812661

Directions: A1(M) junction 6 or 7. Signposted from the motorway

Public transport: Train to Stevenage and then taxi

Distance: 35 miles   **Travel time:** 1 hour

Opening: Daily (except Mondays) from 27th May to 4th September, and most of April. Weekends only in the rest of May and September. Closed 30th June to 3rd July. House and gardens 12.00noon-5.00pm, Park and Fort Knebworth 11.00am-5.30pm

Prices: All inclusive entry £4.50 adult, £4.00 children, under-3's free. Park, Fort and gardens only £3.50 per person, under-3's free, and family tickets £12.00 (4 people)

Nappy changing facilities: no   **Restaurant facilities:** ✓

High chairs: ✓ (no straps)   **Dogs:** Park and Fort only

Pushchair-friendly: ✓ (not house)

Nearby: Hatfield House (see page79)

Syon Butterfly House & Park

Look!
Look!
Look!

ON A COLD OR DULL DAY, A VISIT TO THE BUTTERFLY House, with its warm, humid atmosphere and brightly-coloured tropical flowers, takes some beating. When you first walk in, it takes a few minutes until your eyes adjust to the fact that there are butterflies everywhere. Fluttering through the air, sitting lazily stretching their wings on paths and foliage, hidden in leaves, big ones, small ones, if you start trying to point out every single one you see you will rapidly go into manic overdrive! Although on bright and sunny days you will see more butterflies, even on a dull day the sheer number there is quite amazing with a minimum of 500 on display at any one time, and up to sixty different species. Of course the colours are fantastic, vivid oranges, yellows, viridians, in a huge variety of stripes, spots and leopard skins. And as for size, ranging from about an inch across, to the huge Owl butterflies (about five inches) and Giant Atlas Moths (a stupendous seven inches).

At first it can be a bit of a shock when butterflies settle on you – but you soon get used to it!

The butterflies are all housed in a large greenhouse, ☞

which is subdivided into several sections. There is a small stream running through, with little bridges and pools with terrapins and fish. All captivate small children. The wishing well, which encouraged them to roll coins down to land into the water with a satisfying 'plop', was found to be highly diverting! There are archways laden with tropical blossom, pergolas, and benches where you can sit and watch,

> **"It takes a few minutes until your eyes adjust to the fact that there are butterflies everywhere"**

and try to match the butterflies you can see with those on the identification charts. Identification leaflets are on sale in the shop for 60p each, or you can use the boards inside the butterfly house. Exotic fragrances meander in the heavy air. The emerging cages near the entrance give the chance to watch butterflies coming out from the pupal stages, and you can also see caterpillars on the underside of some leaves (staff are happy to help out with finding caterpillars, and with identification problems).

Most of the butterflies are in the tropical sections. However, from May to September, British butterflies are in display in an adjoining area. At the exit is a small insect gallery: giant millipedes, lizards, tarantulas and the like. Toddlers really needed to be lifted up for a good view here. There is also a very good shop, with small toys, wall charts and books, on a general nature theme.

A visit to the Butterfly House may take from one to two hours. However, there is quite a lot more to do in the vicinity so a day passes easily. Syon Park is worth visiting at the same time as the butterflies – fifty-five acres of Capability Brown landscaped parkland, which make a very pleasant walk at any time of year. There is a large lake running through the middle (beware – it is unfenced), with a few ducks, many fine and interesting trees, and paths suitable for pushchairs. A short miniature railway runs at weekends and bank holidays during the summer, and there is plenty of room to picnic. Should it rain, you could always retreat to the conservatory! Although probably not suitable for children, Syon House itself is open from Easter to September, and there is also a large garden centre, National Trust shop, art shop and wholefood shop, as well as restaurant facilities. In the summer the Koi shop often has exhibits of huge fish in large pools outside.

Look!
Look!
Look!

FACT FILE

Address: London Butterfly House, Syon Park, Brentford, Middlesex
....
Telephone: 0181 560 7272
....
Directions: Take the South Circular to Kew Bridge, then turn left down the A315 towards Twickenham. Signposted 'Syon House'.
....
Public Transport: Train from Waterloo or Clapham Junction, to Kew Bridge station, then 237 or 267 bus to Brentlea Gate (50 yards to pedestrian entrance)
....
Distance: 12 miles   **Travel time:** 30-45 minutes
....
Opening: Summer 10.00am-5.00pm, winter 10.00am-3.30pm. Every day except Christmas and Boxing Days. Syon Park Gardens open 10.00am-6.00pm or dusk, seven days a week
....
Prices: Butterfly House £2.60 adults, £1.60 children. Under 3' free. Family ticket (2 adults, 2 to 4 children) £6.90
....
Nappy changing facilities: Table in ladies toilets in Patio Cafe
....
Restaurant facilities: ✓ in the Patio cafe, adjacent to park entrance
....
High chairs: ✓   **Dogs:** No   **Pushchair-friendly:** ✓
....
Nearby: Kew Gardens (see page 144), Kew Bridge Steam museum (weekends only)

Somewhat Historical
Castles, Cottages And Commoners

Amberley Industrial Museum
"Ding, ding, ding – hold on tight!"

YOU WON'T OFTEN GET THE CHANCE TO RIDE ON THE top deck of a 1920's open top bus, so Amberley is almost worth a trip just for that. However, with over 20 further displays and working exhibits, plus lots of other attractions in the area, there is plenty to do, so plan to set off early and have a really full day here.

The museum consists of a series of traditional trade and crafts workshops, dotted about a 36 acre site in a reclaimed chalk pit in the beautiful South Downs countryside. There is a blacksmith, a cobbler, a clay pipe maker, a potter's workshop, and a woodworking shop, to name just a few of the attractions.

Most are peopled with volunteers working with traditional tools, who are all extremely helpful and enthusiastic – see if you can resist your children's demands for a clay bubble pipe once they've seen the compelling demonstration! The displays exhibit a meticulous attention to detail, and are fascinating for adults. It is a bit like stepping into a Sunday afternoon black and white film. Whilst young children may not appreciate the niceties of the re-created world, they will love the bustle, and older children will love to find craftsmen at work; chiselling, sanding, scraping.

You can hop
on and off the
open-topped
bus or ride
around the
site as often
as you like

It's the bus and train rides that really make
Amberley special for young children. The bus is
wonderful. It leaves from outside the tearooms every
half an hour for a 10-minute ride around the ☞

whole museum. Stopping at a number of key points, it gives a you a chance to get your bearings whilst feeling the wind in your hair and the sun on your face. A conductor comes around to collect 'fares' (you can give a donation) and hands out old-fashioned bus tickets. Meanwhile the workman's train is on a narrow gauge railway, and gives a short steam ride through the woods in an open trailer (enclosed carriages also available). At the end of the line there is a railway museum, which includes a higgledy-piggledy assortment of steam engines and bits and pieces, ideal for scrambling all over if you are two or three years old!

"Younger children will love the bustle, and the older ones will enjoy finding craftsmen at work; chiselling, sanding and scraping"

Our children also enjoyed the water pump display – plenty of opportunities to get your feet splashed here – and the electricity museum, which had buttons to press and levers to pull.

From the far end of the railway line it is about a 30-minute walk back to the tearoom and entrance, a pleasant stroll which takes you past most of the exhibits. There is also a nature trail which runs above, through the woods, and offers a chance to admire the numerous wild flowers and wildlife that have colonised the chalk pits since their closure in the 1960's. The trail is not accessible with a pushchair, but the rest of the museum is.

The Special Events days offer extra attractions – vintage car rallies, bus rallies, motorbike rallies, which are sure to appeal to most children, and which sometimes offer chances for extra rides. These days are often busy, but additional facilities are laid on. They are mostly held in the summer months, but telephone to get details of dates. There are also Santa Special Sundays during December.

The tearoom serves hot drinks, sandwiches and

limited hot meals. As an alternative you could try the Bridge Inn pub just down the road from the museum (be careful – the road is very busy), which has a garden, or the nearby Brasserie. You can picnic in lots of spots inside the museum, but why not walk along the banks of the nearby River Arun and spread yourselves out by the water?

Somewhat Historical

Finally, if you have time, take a river boat trip from the bridge by the museum, either to Arundel and beyond (see Fact File), or to Amberley village (45-minute cruises, available from April to mid October).

FACT FILE

Address: Amberley Museum, Houghton Bridge, Amberley, Sussex
....
Telephone: 01798 831370
....
Directions: Between Storrington and Arundel on the B2139. Follow the brown Industrial Museum signs from either the A24 or the A29
....
Public transport: Trains every hour from Victoria to Amberley . The museum is directly opposite the station. Joint rail and admissions ticket available. River boats run to Amberley from Arundel and Littlehampton in July and August (01243 265792)
....
Distance: 55 miles   **Travel time:** One hour 30 minutes
....
Opening: From end of March to end of October, Wednesday to Sunday (and Bank Holiday Mondays) 10.00am-6.00pm. Open daily during school holidays from Easter to end of October
....
Prices: Adults £4.50, children £2.10. Under 5's free. Family ticket £11.50 (2 adults and up to 3 children)
....
Nappy changing facilities: ✓ (limited)   **Restaurant facilities:** ✓
....
High chairs: No   **Dogs:** ✓ on leads   **Pushchair-friendly:** ✓
....
Nearby: Arundel Castle (telephone 01903 883136)

Bodiam Castle

"This castle hath a pleasant seat . . ."

FOR THE VERY IMAGE OF A FAIRY TALE CASTLE COME TO Bodiam. It is everything children imagine a castle to be. For adults, visiting on a quiet day, maybe at dusk as rainclouds gather, you may feel a tingle in your spine as you picture Macbeth and his wife plotting the demise of Duncan . . .

Bodiam is a small moated medieval castle, little more than an arrow's flight from Hastings. It has the classic square shape with round towers at each corner, beloved of children's drawings. Many of its walls, battlements and stairways are intact, making it a fine place for children to explore. Be prepared for them to end up pretty filthy at the end of the day!

Approaching the castle on a wooden bridge over the wide moat, enormous goldfish and greedy ducks welcomed us as opposed to archers and burning oil. Once you've walked under the portcullis and through the gatehouse you are inside a grassy courtyard surrounded on all sides by the thick external walls. Low remains of internal walls are dotted around – beckoning scrambling up and jumping off, whilst the towers with their wide windowsills and keyhole-shaped slit windows overlooking the moat offer plenty of scope for peering out at imaginary raiders.

The scale of the castle is very manageable, and there are plenty of nooks and crannies that small children will delight in

Do brave the climb up the narrow spiral staircases to the upper floors. On each of the four levels in the south-east tower

you'll discover a circular room with a fireplace and narrow windows, plus medieval toilets which apparently empty straight down into the moat below! There are great views of the surrounding countryside from the top, although those with no head for heights might find the 'machicolations' a bit perturbing! (holes with sheer drops down into the moat – used to drop stones or other evil items onto attackers below). We enjoyed counting the stairs – "thirteen, fourteen, three and a half, four, eighteen five, six" (there were actually 59!) – but they are very steep and uneven so be prepared for a fair amount of carrying and supervision. Pushchairs can get around most of the castle with some ingenuity, but decidedly not the upper levels! Our children had a whale of a time scrambling out of the tiny windows which are just below the level of the courtyard. They also greatly enjoyed throwing money into the spectacular well at the base of the south-east tower. Make sure you have some foreign coins or small change! Most areas are safely fenced where necessary, but you do need to keep an eye on very young children.

Somewhat Historical

"You may feel a tingle in your spine as you picture Macbeth and his wife plotting the demise of Duncan . . ."

The most impressive feature of the castle is its state of preservation. You can really get a feel of what it would have been like to live here all those years ago. Watch the two short well-produced videos on the way round: one showing a knight preparing himself for battle with full-plate armour, and the other re-living life in a medieval castle. Off-season days you'll be likely to have the castle almost to yourself, however in the summer it is a wonderful place for picnics on the grassy slopes below the castle. You don't have to go into the castle, so if you'd prefer just to look at it from afar you can (you'll have to pay the car parking fee of 50p). Spread out your meal ☞

under the noble oaks overlooking the jousting field –
now occupied by sheep rather than gallant knights.
Or stroll along the bridleway which runs alongside.

There is a pleasant restaurant next to the car park.
It has a south facing terrace with tables overlooking
the river. There is also a shop selling National Trust
gifts and a small museum by the castle entrance,
complete with a model of the castle.

Watch out for special events – medieval theme
days, longbow displays and Easter Egg and
Christmas cracker hunts, to name a few.

FACT FILE

Address: Bodiam Castle, Near Robertsbridge, East Sussex

Telephone: 01580 830436

Directions: Take the A21 towards Hastings from junction 5 of the
M25. Turn off at Flimwell towards Hawkshurst, and the castle is
signposted from Hawkshurst

Public transport: none

Distance: 55 miles **Travel time:** One hour 30 minutes

Opening: All year (except Xmas) daily 10.00am–6.00pm or dusk.
Closed Mondays November to April, and occasionally for other periods

Prices: £2.50 adults, £1.30 children. Under-5's free

Nappy changing facilities: ✓ **Restaurant facilities:** ✓

High chairs: ✓ **Dogs:** No (on leads in grounds)

Pushchair-friendly: ✓

Nearby: Historic Rye is great for tea shops!

The Chiltern Open Air Museum

Somewhat Historical

WE COULDN'T HAVE CHOSEN A WORSE DAY TO VISIT the Chiltern Open Air Museum: it wasn't just raining — it was pouring! Although undoubtably better in fine weather, it is a fascinating place, with plenty of shelter to drop into if the rain gets too much!

The Museum is a collection of 25 buildings from around Buckinghamshire that have been saved from demolition. Whilst they give a real insight into the lives and work of a rural community in the past, what is most appealing is the collection's variety and quirkiness. One of the first buildings you see is the Edwardian loo (or to give it its proper name – the Caversham Public Convenience), winner of a 'loo of the year' award! There is also a whole range of different farm buildings including a complete Victorian farmyard, barns, a granary, a shepherd's van and a forge, but more unusually you can visit a 1940's prefab to provide a glimpse of more recent history and an Iron Age house to take you right back to grass roots.

The ticket office is located within the 'Blythe Road Pavilion' which has an extensive display about the museum. Both here and throughout the museum one of the things ☛

History is brought to life on many days as volunteers don period costumes and do traditional tasks

that made our visit enjoyable was the 'Blitz spirit' of the many volunteer helpers who staff the various buildings and who are delighted to talk about the museum and its exhibits. Given that many of them are elderly it is a bit like an oral history lesson. There are plenty of opportunities for the children to enjoy themselves too, including a nature trail (carpeted with bluebells in spring), and farm animals as well as the buildings themselves to run riot in and explore. Indeed, our daughter's favourite experience here (apart from the Eccles cake in the cafe) was chasing after the sheep, although I'm not sure how much fun the sheep thought it was! The numerous ducks, hens, cattle (and new-born calf when we were there) and carthorses in the farm area really make the site live and breathe. On many days everything is further brought to life with workers and craftsmen in period costumes, carrying out their tasks in the traditional way; for example a blacksmith, a spinner and farm workers. There is almost always something going on.

"One of the first buildings you see on entry is the Edwardian loo", winner of a 'loo of the year' award!"

Despite the joys of the Edwardian loo, facilities are a bit limited – no nappy changing areas or mother's room. However, we were assured by a very friendly and informative gentlemen on the information desk that they were in the process of putting in some more toilets halfway round the site and that these would include family facilities. Similarly the cafe is a relatively basic affair offering a small selection of snacks and cakes with some occasional hot dishes such as soup. What the facilities lack in sophistication however is more than compensated for by the goodwill and enthusiasm of the staff. There is a small playground for children but the main attraction for toddlers is exploring the buildings, whilst for older children it is to follow the nature trail and make use of the educational material. Pushchairs can be taken everywhere, including the nature trail. You can picnic unrestrictedly – but the car park is pleasant and opens an hour before the museum, so you can picnic there too.

Somewhat Historical

There are a range of special events held through the year, particularly at weekends, to make it additionally attractive. Planned events include a Family Day, a Medieval weekend, a Taste of the 1940's day, and a Victorian Christmas.

FACT FILE

Address: Newland Park, Gorelands Lane, Chalfont St Giles, Bucks

Telephone: 01494 871117

Directions: M40 junction 1, take the A413 towards Chalfonts and follow the brown museum signs. From M25 junction 17 take the A405 and A412 and follow the brown cart signs

Public transport: Chalfont & Latimer train and tube station, then taxi

Distance: 25 miles **Travel time:** 45 minutes

Opening: April to the end October, Wednesdays to Saturdays, 2.00pm-6.00pm. Car park opens 1 hour before museum

Prices: Adult £3.00, children £2.50, under-5's free. Family ticket (2 adults, 2 children) £10.00

Nappy changing facilities: No (planned) **Restaurant facilities:** ✓

High chairs: No **Dogs:** ✓ on leads **Pushchair-friendly:** ✓

Nearby: Chalfont Shire Horse Centre (01494 872304), and Bekonscot model village (see page 92)

Fort Luton & Kent Life Museum
"Slugs and snails and puppy dogs' tails"

FORT LUTON IS AN 'EXPERIENCE' – GREAT IF YOU LIKE dark tunnels replete with ghastlies and ghouls. Unfortunately many children do! Built in the nineteenth century the Fort's remaining buildings are tunnels and underground arches in what I can only describe as 'pill-box' military architecture style i.e. not particularly gracious. However, it has now been restored and re-opened, and filled with a real 'dogs dinner' of models and relics. The sort that many young children find absolutely fascinating (although adults will probably find quite repellent!). Home-made models, models rescued from TV and film sets, models discovered lurking in garages and attics, model railways, model villages, robots, monsters, space invaders – you name it, they are all scattered around the Fort somewhere! There is a doll and toy museum, a

Children enjoy feeding ducks, whether the setting is historical or not!

penny arcade (come with old 10p pieces if you want to see some of the displays in action), and a new soft-play area. This extraordinary melange seems to keep children whooping with delight for hours.

Somewhat Historical

Apart from the indoor 'attractions' there are several things to do out in the four-and-a-half-acre grounds: an adventure playground, pets corner (with the ugliest turkey I've ever seen), duck pond, moat walk and picnic areas.

The facilities are adequate, but a bit basic. There is a nappy changing mat in the Ladies loo, a cafe serving hot food and cakes and with one high chair, and a gift shop.

The Fort makes a weird day out, but to make it worth the trip you should combine it with a visit to the nearby Kent Life museum, near Maidstone, which with its fresh air and open spaces will be a good antidote to Fort Luton's subterranean tunnels. The museum is set in 26 acres of rural land overlooking the River Medway, and consists of restored buildings, exhibitions and displays which re-create and glorify rural life in times past in ☛

this county, the 'Garden of England'. It runs alongside Allington Lock where boats are moored and ducks paddle leisurely. The whole place has a quiet rural feel and tranquil atmosphere, especially mid-week.

Our children's favourites are the re-constructed hop-pickers huts where adults can wonder at the primitive conditions endured by the annual influx of hop-pickers from London, whilst children play house in their shacks. Then there is the eighteenth century Vale Farm barn which is crammed with displays to keep young children enthralled: farm implements, machinery, and tractors. Traditional crafts such as carpentry, weaving, blacksmithing, stained glass making and potting are regularly demonstrated, whilst seasonal farming activities are always on show – the grand finale being the hop-picking which takes place over the Harvest Weekend, which visitors can arrange to participate in, if the fancy really takes them!

"The extraordinary melange at Fort Luton keeps children whooping with delight"

Being a farm there are animals to admire too, notably Rosie the Shire horse, lambs, goats, rabbits and guinea pigs. These are all kept in a farmyard, with plenty of stroking and holding opportunities. There is also a wooden pig which makes a popular scrambling post, whilst for more lengthy assaults there is a new venture playground.

The 'Darling Buds of May' exhibition has lorries

and a tractor, as well as re-creations of the Larkin family rooms; a bit over the heads of most young children, but ours enjoyed clambering on the truck!

Somewhat Historical

The tearooms are very pleasant, licensed, and offer food and drinks, which you can eat inside or take out into the gardens. There is a picnic area next to the tearooms, and lots of space to have a picnic anywhere in the fields. Special events to watch out for include an Easter Chicken hunt, a St George's dragon hunt, a Kent Cider and Apples day, family days and a folk festival.

FACT FILE

Addresses: Fort Luton, Magpie Hall Road, Chatham, Kent, and Kent Life Museum, Lock Lane, Sandling, Maidstone, Kent
....
Telephone: Fort Luton 01634 813969, Museum 01622 763936
....
Directions: For the Fort the M2 motorway, junction 3, the Chatham exit. Fork right after Toys R Us, and follow signs to the Fort. The Museum is signposted off the M20 motorway (junction 6)
....
Public Transport: Train to Chatham from Victoria, and bus numbers 164 and 64 from bus station to Magpie Hall Road and Fort Luton. Train to Maidstone from Victoria, regular buses from Maidstone East to the Museum, or taxi from the station (about 2 or 3 miles)
....
Distance: 40 miles **Travel time:** 1 hour 30 minutes
....
Opening: Fort, every day except Christmas and Boxing Day 10.00am-6.00pm or dusk. Museum, from Easter to end of October, every day from 10.00am-5.30pm
....
Prices: Fort Luton £2.75 adults, £2.00 children aged 4 and over. The Museum £3.00 adults, £1.50 children. Free for under 5's
....
Nappy changing facilities: ✓ **Restaurant facilities:** ✓
....
High chairs: ✓ **Dogs:** ✓ **Pushchair-friendly:** ✓
....
Nearby: Chatham's Historic Dockyards (01634 812551)

Greenwich – The Cutty Sark & The Maritime Museum

"All hands on deck!!"

SHIVER ME TIMBERS, LANDLUBBERS! STANDING ON THE wooden decks of the Cutty Sark at Greenwich, and imagining the freezing waves crashing over them at 45 degrees is enough to make you feel seasick, let alone think about climbing aloft to wrestle with salt-encrusted ropes and sails! But that was life aboard this famous sailing ship, now dry-docked in Greenwich Harbour, and, together with the many other local attractions, it makes for a splendid day out.

Greenwich is easy and quick to get to, both in the car and by public transport. If you do come by car, be warned that parking can be difficult; try around the Maritime Museum or Cutty Sark jetty. Also, Greenwich is popular with tourists, and often busy. It is best to get there in the morning, see the Cutty Sark and wander round the streets first, before escaping to the quieter Maritime Museum and Greenwich Park for lunch and the afternoon.

The Cutty Sark is the only surviving tea clipper (a sailing boat to you and me), and was launched in 1869 for the tea trade, and later used on the wool route to Australia. When built she was faster than steam ships, and you'll find lots of friendly guides on board who will willingly tell you (as well as many other things) that this is due to her sails, which were equal in area to 11 tennis courts (a rather bizzare unit of measurement!). Now, with her towering main mast and complex rigging, she is a majestic sight, with wide decks which our children found to be great for tearing about on. They were also thrilled by

Children love
the sheer
quirkiness of
life on board
ship

the steep ladder stairs, and awkward little doorways.
The ship's Golden Rule of "one hand for the ship and
one hand for yourself" is worth remembering!
However, the ship is absolutely no good for
pushchairs, so take backpacks for non-walkers.

The ship is filled 'plumb to the gun'ls' with ☞

exciting things for young children – highlights being the lurid figurehead collection in the lower hold, the Captain's cabin, the rope-handled buckets on deck, the massive wheel (actually used to steer around Cape Horn), and the crew quarters and bunks (trying them for size was very popular). On some Sundays you may be lucky enough to catch a troupe of shanty-singers whose lively songs make a great atmosphere. (The words have obviously been cleaned up from the original bawdy sailors' ditty!) There is also a ship shop selling charts, posters, models and guides.

The nearby Maritime Museum has lovely grounds you can walk around for free, with massive 32-pounder guns (great to climb on) and a playground with a very popular wooden 'barge'. Inside the museum are exhibitions of Britain's maritime history: model ships, barges, Nelson's uniform and so on. The pirates exhibition is tremendous for children: it has been re-opened by popular demand, but is only temporary unfortunately. On Saturday and Sunday afternoons Captain Tugboat does storytelling sessions on the 1905 steam paddle tugboat.

Greenwich has lots of other things to do. The craft market on Saturdays and Sundays has a myriad of brightly coloured stalls selling clothes, wooden toys, and all sort of other, good-quality craftware. It can be crowded.

"The Cutty Sark's sails were equal in area to 11 tennis courts!"

Greenwich Park is extensive, has good views, and is very hilly and great for running up and down. Donkey rides are available at the top of park (Shooters Hill) on some days, and you can also visit the Old Royal Observatory which has a huge digital clock, and a hands-on science station for children. There is a cafe in the park. Guided walks around Greenwich, lasting about an hour to an hour and a half, are run by the Tourist Office in Greenwich Church Street (Telephone 0181 858 6169, prices from £4.00, under-14's free).

Somewhat Historical

There are plenty of choices for eating in Greenwich. We recommend the Bosun's Whistle restaurant in the Maritime Museum which is not too busy, and has some high chairs with straps. It offers hot snacks, cakes, drinks, ices and sandwiches. The Pier cafe, on the harbour, is cheap for drinks and snacks, and you can watch the boats going up and down the Thames.

FACT FILE

Address: Cutty Sark, King William Walk, Greenwich, London

Telephone: 0181 858 3445 (Cutty Sark) and 0181 312 6602 (Maritime Museum)

Directions: Take the South Circular, A202, following signs to Greenwich on the A206

Public Transport: Frequent trains from Charing Cross, Waterloo East, Cannon Street and London Bridge (about a 20-minute ride). Boats from Westminster, Charing Cross or Tower piers, about every 30 minutes (telephone 0171 930 4097)

Distance: 15 miles **Travel time:** 45 minutes

Opening: Daily except 24th, 25th and 26th December. Monday to Saturday 10.00am-6.00pm summer (April to September), and 10.00am-5.00pm winter. Sundays and Bank Holidays from 12noon (Cutty Sark) and 2.00pm (Maritime Museum)

Prices: Cutty Sark, Adults £3.25, children £2.25, under-7's free Museum, Adults £3.95, children £2.95, under-7's free

Nappy changing facilities: ✓ (Museum) **Restaurant facilities:** ✓

High chairs: ✓ **Dogs:** No **Pushchair-friendly:** ✓

Nearby: Walk along the river to the Thames barrier

Leeds Castle

Something for everyone: lovely grounds, a maze, avairy and a stunning castle

WHO HASN'T HEARD OF LEEDS CASTLE, OR "THE loveliest castle in the world" as it is often referred to? Although young children may be oblivious to the undoubted beauty of the castle and its setting, there is plenty for them to see in the grounds whilst you muse romantically, and lots of space for them to run about. A word of caution

Somewhat Historical

though, there are several unfenced streams and lakes in the grounds, which, albeit extremely scenic, do mean that you have to keep your eye on toddlers. However, on a sunny day, it would take a lot to beat a visit here.

From the entrance and car park follow the path through the woodland garden to the castle itself, about a 20-minute walk. The path is well-maintained, with several little wooden bridges, and easily negotiable with a pushchair. Carpeted with daffodils and narcissi in the spring, the gardens are very attractive at any time of the year. Our children were thrilled by the Duckery – an area of small ponds and streams created out of the River Len, and full of all sorts of wildfowl roaming freely on the banks and in the water. Try telling your children not to chase the ducks (we weren't very successful!). A certain amount of agility and nimble footedness on your part may be required here if you don't want an extremely wet and muddy toddler.

When you are about three-quarters of the way through the gardens you get your first view of the castle rising mysteriously and majestically from the waters of the lake. It is a wonderful sight. As you walk up to the castle entrance you can decide whether you want to go in or not. A tour of the various rooms and galleries (including state rooms, bedrooms, a wine cellar, and chapel) with the associated halls, staircases, corridors and courtyards would probably take about an hour, and is unlikely to appeal to young children. You are not permitted to take pushchairs inside and must leave them at the castle entrance, where someone will keep an eye on them.

We stayed outside in the sun and fresh air. Carry on walking beyond the castle and along the side of the lake to a visitor area which has special attractions for children: the most interesting being the aviary and maze. The aviary has a host of merrily ☛

squawking parakeets, cockatoos and parrots (or are they all the same thing?). On the whole, children can easily see into the cages to get a good look. There are also huge carp and terrapins in pools.

No pushchairs are allowed into the maze, so be prepared to carry your children or persuade them to walk. It is definitely worth going in, if you can manage it. The maze is a mass of hedged paths, leading, if you are successful at finding your way, to a mound in the middle. This is a great vantage point to jeer at members of your party who haven't got there yet. The mound is, in fact, a hollow dome containing a grotto, which provides an exciting alternative way out of the maze. Although the steps and corridors are very uneven, we had great fun descending into its gloomy depths, and the imaginative and surprising decor (serpents, underworld beasts, skeletons and the like) provoked shrills of glee.

> **"The castle rises mysteriously and majestically from the waters of the lake"**

The Culpepper garden is also worth a stroll. It is a small walled garden next to the aviary, with a profusion of old English cottage garden flowers and herbs. The brick paths and low box-hedged flower beds are a delight to walk in, or run around playing hide and seek in, depending on your preference (and age!). Finally, there is a greenhouse, which is warm and full of exotic blooms, and a vineyard, home to the vines which produce the Leeds Castle wine.

Refreshments are provided in Fairfax Hall, which is a spacious and magnificently-timbered seventeenth century barn located half way between the castle and aviary. Hot and cold food and teas are served, at reasonable prices. The courtyard outside is very pleasant, with benches and tables should you wish to sit and enjoy the sunshine. You can picnic in a designated picnic spot near the main entrance to the garden.

A gift shop, bookshop, and nappy changing facilities are set around the sides of the Fairfax Hall courtyard.

Somewhat Historical

The castle puts on special events throughout the year. The Easter Egg hunt through the grounds is great fun for children, and they would probably also enjoy the hot air balloon and vintage car festival the first weekend in June. During half-terms a cast of actors perform re-enactions of life in the castle, which older children should appeicate.

FACT FILE

Address: Leeds Castle, Maidstone, Kent

Telephone: 01891 800680

Directions: 4 miles east of Maidstone, just off junction 8 of the M20. Signposted from the motorway

Public Transport: Train from Victoria to Bearsted station, with a ten minute coach transfer from Bearsted station on castle open days. All inclusive tickets (train, coach and admission) are available (telephone 0171 620 1032). You can also get a National Express coach from Victoria Station, telephone 0171 730 0202)

Distance: 40 miles **Travel time:** 1 hour 30 minutes

Opening: All year. From 10.00am-5.00pm from March onwards, and from 10.00am-3.00pm in winter. Closed the day before special events and Christmas Day

Prices: Park £5.50 adults, £3.30 children. Castle and park £7.30 adults, £4.80 children . Under-5's free. Family tickets available

Nappy changing facilities: ✓ **Restaurant facilities:** ✓

High chairs: ✓ **Dogs:** No **Pushchair-friendly:** ✓

Nearby: Kent Life Museum (see page 126)

Weald & Downland Open Air Museum

ALTHOUGH 'RURAL ARCHITECTURE' MAY NOT SOUND like the most thrilling way to amuse young children, this award-winning museum falls into the category of 'fascinating for adults plus safe letting-off steam potential for children' and makes a great day out.

This 'museum' is unlike any other museum you may have visited. For a start it is in the open air – 55 acres of gorgeous countryside to be precise, and you (and, in particular, your children) are free to wander, explore and play hide and seek without fear of breaking anything. The museum consists of over 30 rescued historical buildings from the South of England, which have been faithfully and meticulously re-erected. The result is a delightful and informative taste of what the environment of rural and small-town England used to be like to live and work in.

> **"The 'museum' is unlike any other you may have visited"**

There are two suggested routes to follow through the museum, and you can comfortably fit in both in a day, or just about in one afternoon. The shorter, red route takes about half an hour to one hour, and takes in the museum shop (selling gifts, children's colouring books, posters and booklets), several re-created artisan workshops, a working water mill, and millpond, as well as other shops, houses and other buildings from the 15th to 19th century. Highlights of this route include the brick house, where you can play making patterns with traditional bricks, and the water mill, where you can watch the wheat being ground between huge grit millstones into creamy coloured stoneground flour. Both the end product, the flour, and the ingoing wheat are on sale at the mill. The latter is sold as duck food (25p a bag), for the many varieties of ducks and geese who live noisily on the adjacent millpond.

The longer, green route takes anything upwards of an hour and a half, and is a lovely walk through the valley bottom and surrounding woodland. Like the red route you can do it with a pushchair. It takes in traditional cottages and barns, a village school, and shepherds' huts, as well as a re-created charcoal-burners camp, and the impressive medieval Bayleaf Farm. The farm in particular is well worth a visit, with its authentic wood fire in the centre of the hall, where candle-making was in progress when we visited. It also has traditional farm gardens and animals, including huge wallowing pigs, and William, the Shire horse.

There is a refreshment area near the millpond, selling soup, light lunches, bread rolls (home-made with the flour from the mill), tea and cakes. It is closed November to March. You can eat inside a nearby cottage, with open window slats letting in sparrows, which our daughter had great fun chasing! There are also plenty of picnic tables and benches around, or you may eat your own food anywhere in the ☞

You can feed the ducks and geese on the millpond with wheat from the adjacent working mill

grounds, except inside the houses (it attracts mice).

Because you can always duck into a nearby building this is a day out with wet weather potential, although if it is really pouring continuously childrens' opportunities to run about outside may be a bit curtailed! When we went in October there was a lovely smell of wood smoke drifting through the air, and autumn leaves to kick through. It can get busy in the summer, as it is popular with school parties, but there is plenty of space to escape into. There are lots of special events; many geared towards children.

FACT FILE

Address: Singleton, Chichester, Sussex

Telephone: 01243 811348

Directions: A3, then A286 to Midhurst and Chichester. Signposted from Singleton village (midway between Midhurst and Chichester)

Public Transport: Train to Chichester from Waterloo, then number 260 bus to Singleton, which runs about every 40 minutes

Distance: 50 miles   **Travel time:** 1 hour 30 minutes

Opening: Daily from March to end of October, 11.00am-5.00pm. Weekends and Wednesdays (and 26th December to 2nd January) from 1st November to end of February, 11.00am-4.00pm

Prices: £4.20 adults, £2.10 children, under-5's free. Family tickets £11.00 (2 adults, 2 children)

Nappy changing facilities: ✓ at entrance

Restaurant facilities: ✓

High chairs: No   **Dogs:** ✓   **Pushchair-friendly:** ✓

Nearby: The Horse and Groom pub in Singleton has a family room and play area. Midhurst is a pretty small town with tea shops. Goodwood Racecourse is within a few miles (01243 774107)

The Sun Has Got His Hat On
Walks And Picnic Spots

The Sun
Has Got
His Hat On

Clifton Hampden

*"All was a-shake and a-shiver, glints
and gleams and sparkles, rustle and
swirl, chatter and bubble"*

REMEMBER THOSE LAZY SUMMER DAYS, DANGLING YOUR
feet in a cool river as the sun baked down?
Clifton Hampden will bring all those memories
flooding back – playing ball in a river meadow,
eating sandwiches and drinking fizzy drinks. The
Thames curves lazily through the bridge, the
meadow spreads out on one side while the village
gardens and small coppices cover
the slight scarp on the other side.
To the south lie the rolling Sinodun
Hills, outriders for the Chilterns,
dominated by the ancient site of
Wittenham Clumps.

**"Spread out your
blanket and open
up the hamper for
a day of bliss on
the river bank"**

Clifton Hampden is a few miles
south of Oxford, four miles east of
Abingdon along the A415. There is a small village
with two pubs (The Plough beside the A415 and The
Barley Mow) and a village shop of the type which is
rapidly becoming extinct (Beware! ice-cream may be
available. . .). Turning south off the A415 (signposted
Long Wittenham), you rapidly cross the old ☞

Ramble along the grassy banks of the Thames, until you find your own private cove

bridge, with its many arches. The road swings to the right, around a picturesque thatched pub, the Barley Mow, on your right and a car park appears on your left. Leave the car here and walk back along the road to the bridge. It is a popular spot with local people and you should have no trouble finding the stile through to the meadow on your right (just a couple of hundred yards from the car park). Immediately you are in a broad grassy area – pitch up here if you wish, or walk on along the riverside towpath (public right of way) and stop further down. Some fields will have cows grazing, but they generally seem incurious of their visitors. The river bank here has been eroded to form a series of miniscule 'coves', many of which boast sand or fine gravel bottoms. Ideal for a little paddling, but do be careful. The river generally runs slower and calmer on this side but the Thames is a powerful river and children could easily be swept away.

There are few specific facilities for families, but what do you need in a rural picnic spot? There are toilets in the car park, but they are basic and we have found them vandalised on occasion. Both pubs welcome families and have outside playground areas. The village shop stocks basic necessities, soft drinks etc.

For a wider selection of goodies Abingdon is probably your best bet. Indeed, you could do worse than plan to spend part of your day there. It has many attractive buildings in the town centre (pedestrianised) and a wide choice of pubs and restaurants. Other local places to visit include the medieval Abbey in nearby Dorchester and the museum in Long Wittenham. However, I suspect that you will just want to spread out your blanket, get out the bat and ball and open up the hamper for a day of bliss on the river bank.

The Sun Has Got His Hat On

FACT FILE

Address: Clifton Hampden, Long Wittenham, Oxon
....

Telephone: Blissfully none!
....

Directions: The easiest way to get there is probably up the M40 as far as Junction 7 (Milton Common) taking the A329 to Stadhampton and thence to Clifton Hampden either via Drayton St. Leonards or via Chiselhampton and Golden Balls
....

Public Transport: None
....

Distance: 60 miles   **Travel time:** 1 hour 30 minutes
....

Opening: Any sunny day . . .
....

Prices: Free!
....

Nappy changing facilities: No
....

Restaurant facilities: The Barley Mow and Plough pubs
....

High chairs: No   **Dogs:** ✓   **Pushchair-friendly:** ✓
....

Nearby: Oxford, Medieval abbey at Dorchester

Kew Gardens

IF YOU THINK THAT THE ROYAL BOTANIC GARDENS AT Kew are just for ardent plant spotters discussing the merits of different chrysanthemum species, think again, because they are ideal for a day's picnic, and very easy to get to, both by car and by public transport. One of Kew's strongest points for

The exuberant leafiness inside the Palm House is a dramatic contrast to the grassy and wooded gardens outside

those with young children is that it is dog free, which must make it one of the largest pooh-free areas that you can find. Despite being very popular at weekends, you can still find far-flung corners that are to all intents and purposes deserted, and in the week – well, you will almost find the whole gardens at your disposal.

The Sun Has Got His Hat On

A mixture of wide grassed areas and woodland areas, the gardens are very extensive – you'd be hard-pushed to cover everywhere in one day. Although there are some formal flower displays, most of the gardens are pretty wild in character, but do have lovely andwide pushchair-friendly footpaths. There are no nasty 'Keep off the grass' notices, and you can romp at will through shady dells and woody glens. Dotted around are information boards to help you gen up on your general knowledge skills (do you know how many oak trees it took to build a sailing galleon, for example?). Older children get a lot of fun and interest out of these boards. Over at the quieter, far side of the gardens the paths border onto the banks of the Thames, with the requisite fisherman gently passing the day, and the occasional rowing eight . ☞

The leaflet you are given at the entrance marks three suggested walks. Try our favourite – the West Walk which is the quietest, and which has several little shelters and alcoves for playing in. The other walks are the East Walk, which includes the glasshouses and temples, and the North Walk which takes in the 17th century gardens in Kew Palace and those famous lilacs. There is usually

"You can still find far-flung deserted corners in Kew Gardens"

something to see at any time of the year – bulbs, cherry blossom and lilacs in the spring; roses, giant water lilies and bedding plants in the summer; berries and autumn leaves to kick through in October and November; and Holly trees, strawberry trees and camelias in the winter.

Should you tire of wandering in the gardens, there are always the glasshouses to pop into. The largest and most impressive are the Temperate House, where you can spot tangerines, grapefruits and avocados growing, and the steamy Palm House, with coconuts, date palms, bananas and giant bamboo. Both have walkways running high above the floor level so you can look down on the dizzy depths of tangled foliage before descending once again into the undergrowth of exotic scents and heady blooms. You'll have to leave pushchairs down at ground level though. In the basement of the Palm House there is a marine display of algae and fishes. You have to lift up young children to see inside many of the displays here though.

Catering facilities are good in the summer, with a choice of cafes and kiosks selling the usual range of food and drinks. During the winter, there is less choice: during the week only the Orangery restaurant is open. On sunny Sundays you may have to queue up to a quarter of an hour for your food, and be prepared to share your table (and children's table manners!) with an unsuspecting member of the public. By far the best thing to do though is to bring a picnic, spread it out somewhere that takes your fancy, and enjoy the freedom of eating in the fresh air.

The Sun Has Got His Hat On

A couple of final points, as well as the ban on dogs, you are also not allowed to bring bikes, trikes or radios into the gardens, or play ball games. This may be a blessing to some, but a disappointment to others. If you come in the car you will have to park in the surrounding streets and, be warned, it can prove difficult to find somewhere at busy times.

FACT FILE

Address: Royal Botanic Gardens, Kew, Richmond, Surrey

Telephone: 0181 940 1171 (answerphone), 0181 332 5000

Directions: Take the A205, South Circular to Kew, turning off and following the signs to Kew Gardens before you cross Kew Bridge

Public Transport: Trains run from Waterloo to Kew Bridge station approximately every 30 minutes. There is a 10-minute walk across Kew Bridge to the Gardens from the station. Alternatively the District line tube to Kew Gardens - it is then about a 5-minute walk. During summer river boats run from Westminster (0171 930 2062)

Distance: 10 miles   **Travel time:** 30-45 minutes

Opening: Open all the year, except Christmas and New Year's days. 9.30am-5.30pm in the winter, and to 6.00pm in the summer (7.00pm Sundays and Bank Holidays). Glasshouses close at 4.30pm Mondays to Saturdays, and 5.00pm on Sundays

Prices: £4.00 adults, £2.00 children, under-5's free. Family ticket (2 adults and up to 4 children £10.00)

Nappy changing facilities: ✓   **Restaurant facilities:** ✓

High chairs: ✓ (no straps)   **Dogs:** No   **Pushchair-friendly:** ✓

Nearby: Kew Bridge Steam Museum (0101 568 4757)

Polesden Lacey

IF YOU LIKE DREAMING, TRY WANDERING AROUND THE gardens at Polesden Lacey, and muse on how life would have been here ninety years ago – elegant ladies with parasols, fine dresses, delicate dishes, and children safely tucked away with governesses. Then come back to earth with a jolt as your delightful offspring hurtle towards a muddy puddle or go puce in the face as you try to cajole them to put their gloves on.

Polesden Lacey is a beautiful Regency house, formerly owned by the playwright and politician Sheridan, and overlooking a wonderful secluded valley in the midst of Surrey. The grounds, which are very extensive, are great for walking in with children. There are gravel paths through walled rose arbours, formal gardens with iris and lavender separated by box hedges (great for hide and seek), and rolling lawns and terraces with stunning views of the North Downs. The Long Walk, Nuns' Walk and Admiral's walks are short trails through the woodland, fields and terraces that make up the estate. None taking more than half an hour to complete, they provide good routes to leisurely stroll around the grounds. Although somewhat muddy in places after wet weather, they are suitable for pushchairs. The estate is full of little nooks and crannies that most children will delight to explore – our children's favourite is the half-timbered thatched bridge with steps up, and the chance to gaze down at the occasional car passing in the lane below. The bridge leads to an orchard of lime and cherry trees – ideal for picnics.

Owned by the National Trust, Polesden Lacey

"The estate is full of little nooks and crannies that most children will delight to explore"

offers reasonable additional facilities: a restaurant with outside tables situated in a pretty courtyard, a National Trust gift shop (quite a few children's toys and books), and toilets with a nappy change table. There are plenty of good picnic spots to settle in, although picnicing is not allowed on the main lawns around the house. You may also visit the house, but pushchairs would have to be left outside.

The Sun Has Got His Hat On

For a good day out, though, you could have lunch in the many nearby Surrey pubs. We particularly like The White Horse at Shere, which, although not specifically catering for families, does allow children in a side bar. It does good meals, and ☞

Nearby Shere is very picturesque and has ducks to feed in the village stream

has a lovely mellow atmosphere, with wood panelling, old oak beams and log fires in the winter. Shere village is charming — complete with small streets, antique shops, and ducks cavorting in the stream running through the village — the only drawback is the large number of people there at weekends! If you fancy walking from Shere as well as at Polesden Lacey, there are several public footpaths from the village too. Try going up behind the wonderfully quaint village church, and following the paths across the fields.

FACT FILE

Address: Polesden Lacey, Bookham, Near Dorking, Surrey

Telephone: 01372 458203 or 452048

Directions: Located just off the A246 between Leatherhead and Guildford. Signposted from Great Bookham

Public Transport: None

Distance: 30 miles   **Travel time:** 45 minutes by car

Opening: Grounds are open daily all year 11.00am-6.00pm or dusk. The house is open in the afternoons only, and is restricted to certain days. The restaurant is open from 11.00am Wednesday to Sunday, except in January, February and March when it is only open at the weekend. It closes daily from 2.00pm-2.30pm, reopening for tea until 5.30pm in the summer, and 4.30pm in the winter. Last orders 30 minutes before closing

Prices: Grounds only adults £2.50 in the summer, £2.00 in the winter, children half price, and under-5's free. House £2.50, or £3.50 Sundays and Bank Holidays

Nappy changing facilities: ✓   **Restaurant facilities:** ✓

High chairs: ✓   **Dogs:** ✓   **Pushchair-friendly:** ✓

Nearby: Shere village. Walks on the North Downs, around Box Hill

Windsor Town & Great Park

The Sun
Has Got
His Hat On

WINDSOR IS PERFECT FOR A PICNIC AND A REALLY FULL day – wonderful for the long days of summer. There is an almost endless choice of nearby picnic spots – Runnymede by the river; the rural tranquility of the Great Park, where you can often catch polo matches in the summer; or the fields and pastures around Datchet.

As the Thames meanders gently through lush meadows past Windsor, our favourite spot is very close to the centre of Windsor, but is actually over the river in Eton. Cross over Windsor River Bridge to Eton, it is generally quieter than Windsor town there, and walk upstream along the towpath through The Brocas meadow. The broad, open meadow is everything a perfect picnic spot should be: soft, luxurient grass with buttercups, daisies, clover and dandelions, the river gently lapping the banks, and spectacular views of Windsor Castle and Eton College as a backdrop. Sit on the banks and watch everyone messing about in boats – some vigilance is required here if your children are anything like ours – or pick a patch further back in the meadow, where it is more peaceful and shadier. Or just continue walking along the towpath through woods and pastures. Watch out for bicycles on the towpath though, as

> **"The Castle is the largest in England and you can walk around the grounds for free"**

the coaches for the Eton College oarsmen pound along the bank shouting encouragement (or abuse) to the crews! (It may be quieter in a few years time when the controversial new rowing course is built upstream at Dorney, but then there won't be so much entertainment.) ☞

Windsor – great picnic spots by the river, all accoutrements of royalty in the town, and international polo in the Great Park

Alternatively, stay on the Windsor side of the river and walk upstream along the promenade, past fishermen and river boats, towards the Alexandra Gardens. You will see plenty of enthusiastic swans, ducks and geese to feed (if you want to lose your fingers!). About half a mile upstream from the bridge you can picnic in the gardens. There is a small toddler funfair nearby with about five or six rides (£1.00 for four rides). On a really hot day the Alexandra Gardens have the advantage over the Eton side by offering lots of large, shady trees.

The Sun Has Got His Hat On

In Windsor town there is plenty to see and do. The Castle is the largest castle in England, and you can walk around the grounds free. It is open every day (except Garter Day) and can be subject to closure at short notice (01753 831118 to check). The Changing of the Guard is at 11.00am daily from May to early August, and alternate days the rest of the year. If the weather is poor there are many museums – Queen Mary's Dolls House, the Royalty and Empire exhibition at the Windsor & Eton Central station, or perhaps the Household Cavalry Museum.

If you fancy the sights, horse-drawn carriage rides go from the taxi stand outside Windsor castle, but at £19.00 for a half hour trip the cost may be prohibitive. Alternatively try a river boat (£4.20 adults, £2.10 children from one to thirteen years, for a two-hour trip), or an open top bus (01753 855755 for details).

Periodically through the summer Windsor Great Park is the site for international and national polo matches. These would be a day out in themselves. All the glamour of a major sporting event – expensive cars, champagne, strawberries and picnic hampers – but without the crowds that are often so intimidating with young children. Even the busiest events are very accessible. Children are fascinated by the spritely polo ponies, and there are usually horsey exhibitions and trade stands.

Park your car in one of the designated car ☞

parks (approximately £10.00 per car for an international event) and walk up with your picnic to large, free grassy enclosures alongside the field. Alternatively you can pay a lot more to go into one of the stands to rub shoulders with the cognoscenti. In summer, from around the start of May, polo is on every day except Monday, with matches two or three times a week, and major international events three times a year. All are held in the Guards Polo Club in the centre of the Park. Details are obtainable from the Polo Club (01784 434212).

FACT FILE

Address: Windsor, Berkshire

Telephone: 0753 852010 Windsor Tourist Information Centre

Directions: Take either the M4 (junction 6) or M3 (junction 3) motorways. Parking in Windsor town can be difficult - try the station car parks, or along Meadow Lane on the Eton side of the river (in which case take junction 5, the Eton exit off the M4 and approach Eton through Datchet). For the Great Park approach via Egham (junction 13 off the M25), and Old Windsor

Public Transport: Trains from Waterloo to Windsor & Eton Riverside. Also trains from Paddington to Slough, and then a local train to Windsor & Eton Central Station

Distance: 25 miles **Travel time:** 1 hour

Nappy changing facilities: No. Toilets in the station car park in Windsor, and The Brocas car park in Eton

Restaurant facilities: The usual choice of pubs and restaurants

High chairs: In some restaurants

Dogs: ✓ **Pushchair-friendly:** ✓

Nearby: The Courage Shire Horse Centre (01628 824848)

Whitstable

*"But four young Oysters hurried up
All eager for the treat. . . ."*

The Sun
Has Got
His Hat On

FOR A SOMEWHAT DIFFERENT DAY AT THE SEASIDE TO the usual amusement arcades, kiss-me-quick hats and fish and chip bars, come to Whitstable. Easily accessible by train, this quiet and unassuming sea port on the Thames estuary offers a beach, a working harbour, and a Lilliputian-scale village replete with antique shops. All within an environment of wheeling seagulls, distant ships on the horizon, and the distinctive sea smell of rotting seaweed!

The main beach, Tankerton Slopes, is a 15-minute walk from the railway station, or there is plenty of parking space nearby. Although a pebble beach, there are lovely safe grassy slopes sweeping gently down to the promenade, and a wide shelving seashore. With lots of space, groynes to scramble ☞

An old-fashioned seaside resort with an oyster heritage that you can still enjoy

on, and an inexhaustible supply of pebbles to play with, kids can be quite happy for hours and maybe you could even try a swim yourself. There is a small cafe and tearooms, and public loos nearby.

Walking back towards the town and harbour from the beach, along Beach Walk and Tower Parade you pass Whitstable Castle, a nineteenth century folly with attractive gardens, and the Tea Rooms, open Thursdays, Fridays and Sundays, which have gardens overlooking the harbour. The harbour itself is a working port with all the associated bustle of boats, cranes and machinery. The activity, sights and smells are a treat for young children – ours were fascinated by the whelk-shelling conveyor belt, but of course you'll need to be vigilant with respect to sheer drops into the water, quarry lorries, and working equipment. At the east end of the harbour there is an oyster fishery exhibition, with memorabilia and displays of Whitstable's famous oyster industry. You can buy fresh oysters packed to take home, see a live shellfish display, or get your fingers wet in the seashore 'boat pool'.

"The activity, sights and smells of the harbour are a treat for young children"

The town centre has a timeless air about it, and consists of quaint narrow streets, weather-boarded fishermen's houses, and period shops. Some of the narrow pavements can be a bit difficult to negotiate with pushchairs, it must be admitted, but if you leave the High Street and branch down one of the many alleys you will get to the Sea and Island Walls which are easier to walk along with children.

On the High Street is small model railway museum, Chuffa Trains, a 'trainomania' collection of railway artefacts, photographs and model trains. It is up steep stairs, which are again difficult to negotiate with a pushchair, but there is a good children's play area where our children enjoyed pushing the buttons on several model train sets, whilst we looked around the exhibits somewhat more at leisure.

The Sun Has Got His Hat On

If you don't picnic on the beach, family-friendly facilities in the town are a bit hard to come by. We lunched in the Old Neptune pub on the seafront, a very traditional white-painted old pub with wooden chairs and floors. It is one of the historical features of the town itself, worth looking at even if you don't eat there. The food is just burgers and sandwiches, but there is a kids menu for £2.25. It has a small outside patio with tables and chairs.

FACT FILE

Address: Whitstable, near Canterbury, Kent

Telephone: 01227 275482 (information centre)

Directions: Exit the M2 at junction 7, then the A299

Public transport: Trains from Victoria station every hour

Distance: 55 miles **Travel time:** 1 hour 30 minutes

Opening: Oyster Exhibition 10.00am-4.00pm daily, except Wednesday, May to September. Chuffa Trains daily, except Sunday, 10.00am-3.00pm, (5.00pm Saturday and school holidays)

Prices: Oyster Exhibition 50p adult, 30p children. Chuffa Trains £1.00 adult, 50p children

Nappy changing facilities: No **Restaurant facilities:** ✓

High chairs: No **Dogs:** ✓

Pushchair-friendly: ✓

Nearby: Blean Bird Park (01227 471666), or Canterbury (cathedral, walks and museums)

Notes

Feedback

PLEASE WRITE TO ME IF YOU HAVE ANY COMMENTS OR suggestions to make about the trips included in Days Out With Kids. Every letter received will be entered in a draw, and the first ten out of the hat will receive a copy of the next edition absolutely free.

Janet Bonthron
Days Out With Kids
Two Heads Publishing
12a Franklyn Suite
The Priory
Haywards Heath
RH16 3LB

OTHER BOOKS AVAILABLE FROM TWO HEADS PUBLISHING

The Bookshops of London
A comprehensive guide to bookshops in and around London. The lively and informative descriptions are presented in twenty-three subject classifications, from Antiquarian to Women. *Pbk, 170pp, £6.99.*

The Organic & Sustainable Farm Holiday Guide
Details of organic and sustainable farms in the British Isles, Ireland and France offering green holidays with a difference. All the information you need to find the type of farm, accommodation, facilities or healthy produce you are looking for. *Pbk, 184pp, £7.99.*

Breathing Spaces
– Bike rides within easy reach of London
Twenty-four bike rides, easily reached from London by car or by train. A mix of on-and off-road routes, all day rides for mountain bikers and tourers, leisurely country lanes and family rides. With route maps, details of places to see and where to stop for refreshments. *Pbk, 170pp, £7.99.*

Cox's Rural Rides
A choice of thirty-six bike rides in the south-east. The choice of tours ranges from short excursions to challenging day trips - routes can easily be linked to form longer routes. The descriptions include details of places to see, fascinating local history and where to stop for food and drink. *Pbk, 272pp, £8.99.*

Get Lost
This off-road follow-up to Breathing Spaces contains twenty great escapes from London and the suburbs to the countryside. *Pbk, 192pp, £7.99.*

Available from all good bookshops or direct from the publisher plus £1 postage and packing. Two Heads Publishing, 12a Franklyn Suite, The Priory, Haywards Heath, West Sussex, RH16 3LB.